"Karen's book is a must read to be a successful coach, and ar but is struggling to build their b............ ....any useful tips in here, and plenty of 'straight from the horse's mouth' advice from seasoned professionals. I would definitely recommend this as required reading for anyone who wants to build a coaching business on solid foundations. It's easy to read, straightforward. I thoroughly enjoyed it – a useful guide that I will certainly draw on."

– **Wendy Dashwood-Quick**, coach, consultant and author, Resolution Coaching, www.resolutioncoaching.co.uk

"With the release of her new book *The Secrets of Successful Coaches*, Karen Williams has her finger on the pulse of the coaching business today. This is a long-awaited and valuable resource for newly qualified coaches. Many coaches embark with high hopes to launch a successful and profitable practice. Unfortunately many also discover that *hope* is not a viable marketing strategy! This is the point when solid professional advice is vitally needed from those who understand coaching as a business. What is refreshing about this book is its pragmatic approach. Every chapter contains 'golden nuggets' of business advice and simple NLP self-help exercises which can be put to use from day one by novice coaches. I would also recommend *The Secrets of Successful Coaches* as a useful resource for coach-mentors and coach trainings schools, as well as related professions, such as counselling. What could be more valuable or relevant to the new practitioner than a rich depository of insights and stories from the world's top coaches in one book?

As Karen's supervisor, I am especially delighted to see the success of *The Secrets of Successful Coaches*. I have one regret – that this publication was not available when I set up my own coaching practice!"

– **Lisa Rossetti**, coach, mentor and supervisor, Positive Lives, www.positivelives.co.uk

"*The Secrets of Successful Coaches* is an intelligently written book designed to teach you the secrets of becoming a successful coach. It really lives up to the title, the index, and the promise of giving you the secrets of becoming a *successful* coach. It sets a good foundation and builds steadily introducing you to a behind the scenes insight into the minds of experts in the know. I've met thousands of would-be coaches over the years. Without applying the secrets in this book, they will always be would-be coaches. Karen's own success is a testament to the contents of this book. She has lived and breathed the material herself, and it works. Apply what you read, and you will succeed."

– **Richard Scott**, international time management and work-life balance expert, author, coach, and trainer, Smart Inspiration, www.smartinspiration.com

"This is a great book for any business owner whether small or large. The NLP exercises throughout the book help you to realise your beliefs, and confidence, which in putting into practice in your own business can only develop it further. Great resource and an inspiring read which fills you with motivation."

– **Laura Morris**, award winning business woman, Rentabuggy, www.rentabuggy.co.uk

"*The Secrets of Successful Coaches* is well written, easy to understand, useful and relevant. It is a great to dip in and out of, different sections apply at different times and will be a book I regularly refer back to for information and self development. There are lots of really useful ideas to improve your chances of running a successful coaching business. The exercises are easy to complete – often taking just a few minutes – and I found them to be totally relevant for me at this stage of my developing business. I particularly like the section on eliciting values. I've always been very clear on my specialised coaching niche and I have strong values. In the past, I've found that staying true to my own values may not be what the 'experts' think to be the 'right' way forward for my business and, against my gut instinct, I have occasionally got lost following someone else's 'right' way.

I believe that if you don't honour your own uniqueness, you will be setting yourself up to fail. It was really useful to be reminded to regularly check in and update my values to make sure that I am still in alignment."

– **Bridie Nelson**, chronic illness coach-therapist, www.bridienelson.com

"I have found The Secrets of Successful Coaches immensely useful packed with great NLP techniques, some that I have seen before but you have explained it in a clear and concise way. Most coaches will go into coaching because they like to help other people achieve happiness in their lives. Often though this is at the expense of their own success. Coaches can only help people and grow their own business if they approach their practice as a business. It's a little like being on a plane when the air masks deploy. You need to help yourself first before you can help others. The book is packed with practical advice and techniques to boost confidence, awareness and knowledge of how to grow your coaching business successfully (and also add to your coaching toolkit). My personal favourites were how to become an expert in your field and the fantastic advice and interviews from coaches who have already found success. I would definitely recommend *The Secrets of Successful Coaches* to anyone who wants to set up a coaching business and also experienced coaches. I know that I will re read this again and again to ensure I am keeping my own business on the right track and moving forward."

– **Darren Toms**, personal leadership expert, coach and motivational speaker, The Choice, www.darrentoms.com

"*The Secrets of Successful Coaches* is an insightful and inspiring text, championing the growth of all service and creative sectors. It helps business owners to question the approach we might all take for granted whilst celebrating successes, guiding us to think and act in line with our vision and best lives."

– **Lyndsey Whiteside**, public relations consultant, Inspired PR, www.inspiredpr.co.uk

"I have had the pleasure of reading *The Secrets of Successful Coaches* and it was a joy to read. Karen has clearly worked tirelessly amongst top coaches from the UK and the States to bring us their best advice. She set out to give the reader the resources, tips and motivation to create a successful business that fit with their needs and indeed she has been very successful in that quest. I found the exercises particularly helpful and loved her use of motivational quotations throughout the book. It is a very inspiring book and I have no hesitation in recommending it."

– **Lyn Blackledge**, business woman, Lyn's Biz, www.lynsbiz.co.uk

The Secrets of

SUCCESSFUL
COACHES

10 steps to develop a winning business mindset

Karen Williams

Matador
5 Weir Road
Kibworth Beauchamp
Leicester LE8 0LQ, UK
Tel: (+44) 116 279 2299
Fax: (+44) 116 279 2277
Email: books@troubador.co.uk
Web: www.troubador.co.uk/matador

ISBN 978 1848766 372

British Library Cataloguing in Publication Data.
A catalogue record for this book is available from the British Library.

Typeset in Verdana by Troubador Publishing Ltd, Leicester, UK
Printed and bound in Great Britain by TJ International, Padstow, Cornwall

Matador is an imprint of Troubador Publishing Ltd

To all the coaches out there who want to make a difference – enjoy the journey and wishing you the greatest success!

Contents

Foreword

How can I succeed? What on earth do I need to do? Who can help me?

These are just a few variations of the questions any newly-qualified coach will ask themselves as they look down the long of road of success.

Their initial enthusiasm about their new business venture can diminish as they realise just what they need to do to become the success they dreamed about.

It's a problem, in fact...

It's a massive problem. This is why so many (studies indicate 75%+) never really achieve the level of success their level of skills indicates they should reach.

Many coaches are ambling through life, attending networking meetings, playing with the Internet, hoping the phone will ring. Their partners and friends are beginning to think their original negative comments were well founded.

It must stop!

At last – someone who walks the talk! Someone who's been there and done it!

Someone who's not only learned from the best – but taken the lessons, honed and polished them by application to create a system of success for coaches – a system that works!

Karen Williams is now your guide. Take her by the hand, let her lead you to your dreams fulfilled; your goals achieved; your desires accomplished and enjoyed.

Enjoy the journey!

– **Peter Thomson**, The UK's Leading Strategist on Personal and Business Growth, Peter Thomson International Plc, www.peterthomson.com

Acknowledgments

Firstly, without doubt, I would like to thank all of the successful coaching business owners who contributed their time and their knowledge to the production of this book. Thank you to Allison Marlowe, Blaire Palmer, Dawn Breslin, Duncan Brodie, Gladeana McMahon, Hannah McNamara, Marian Way, Michael Neill, Steve Marriott, Suparna Dhar, and Suzy Greaves. I would especially like to thank Allison who has been my coach, mentor, and friend for the last four years and has supported me every step of the way to enable me to transform my own coaching business. I would also like to give an additional mention to Suparna, who has been my friend, supporter and champion since we met during our coaching training in 2006.

Secondly, I would like to acknowledge my own network of amazing and inspirational business owners and leaders who have encouraged me to follow my dreams, including writing this book, and with whom I have forged some great friendships too. I would especially like to mention Tracy Harris, Roberta Jerram, Wendy Wyatt, Rachel O'Reilly, and Lisa Rossetti.

Particular thanks go to Bridie Nelson especially for helping me to get the flow of this book right, and to John Cassidy-Rice of Training Excellence who taught me the NLP skills and supported me during my modelling project. I would like to acknowledge my fellow NLP Master Practitioners including Nick Burnside, Allie Devenney and

Richard Scott, who have provided immense support.

I would also like to thank my parents, Barbara and Ken Legg, for their ongoing support, for being proud of me, and for providing me with additional sets of eyes to get this book finished, which at times felt like a never-ending mission.

Lastly, my special thanks go to my husband, Peter, whose ongoing support and faith in me has kept me going over the last four years of running my business. His unwavering belief has given me the motivation to break through my own barriers, transform my own business and enhance my personal success.

Chapter 1 – Introduction

'If you want to be successful, it's just this simple: Know what you're doing. Love what you're doing. And believe in what you're doing.' – Will Rogers

There are hundreds of thousands of life, business and executive coaches across the world, with numbers increasing dramatically year on year, yet many of them struggle to make a decent living from coaching. Many of these people become a coach because they have a passion to make a difference and to help other people to achieve the life they desire.

However, a coaching qualification alone does not mean that you can run a successful coaching business. The truth is that many coaches give up because they cannot make enough money to live on through coaching. They either struggle to find enough clients to pay the bills or they suffer from feast and famine, which then impacts on their own health, wealth and self-belief. This is not the right mindset to achieve success.

That's not to say that there are not enough clients to go around. Coaching has been one of the fastest growing professions, with increasing publicity through national newspapers, magazines and television programmes. You don't have to be a celebrity or a leader to have a coach; it is becoming more mainstream for individuals across the world in their search for a better and more satisfying life.

I set up my business, Self Discovery Coaching, in 2006, and the one question that has puzzled me for a while now is: *What is the difference between someone who runs a successful coaching business and someone who does not?* Why do some coaches have enough clients and others find it hard to stay afloat?

These are the questions I asked when I carried out research for my Neuro Linguistic Programming (NLP) Master Practitioner modelling project in 2009, and when I decided to model the mindset behind a successful coaching business.

This book itself is an accumulation of my research during this project plus an ongoing sense of curiosity that I would like to share with you. I have had the great fortune of spending time with some of the most successful coaches who I recognise as being at the pinnacle of success in their business. Ordinary people like you and I, who are successful in what they do.

How will this book help you?

If you are a coach running your own business, and you are not yet achieving the success you desire, this book is for you. This book is not a self-help book and it won't teach you the skills to become a great coach, although it aims to provide you with some great business support and is a signpost to additional resources that will help you on your journey.

This book will give you the resources, tips and motivation to create a successful coaching business that fits in with your needs. By modelling coaches who already run successful coaching businesses, you will find out what works and what doesn't work, and learn the secrets of success from those who do it well. And then you can apply these to your own business. As you work your way through the book, you will also undertake a variety of NLP exercises, which will allow you to instil some of the strategies to increase your levels of success. Equally the principles in this book can be adopted by anyone who runs a service-based business to achieve greater success.

What is NLP?

If you ask even the most experienced NLP practitioner, they struggle to answer this question. NLP is often described as an owner's manual for the brain, the study of communication or the study of human excellence. Let me tell you a bit about its history and where it all started.

NLP was born in the 1970s in California when John Grindler, a linguist, and Richard Bandler, a mathematician, set out to identify the difference between the behaviour of people who were competent at a particular skill and those who excelled at it.

They modelled the behaviour of two top psychotherapists, Virginia Satir and Fritz Perls, and Milton Erickson, the world-famous hypnotherapist. Although these individuals had very different styles, they used similar underlying patterns. Following this exercise they designed a model for others to use to improve their performance, to become excellent communicators, and to undergo personal change.

They called it:

- Neuro – because the patterns they discovered were at the level of our neurological thought processes.
- Linguistic – because of the ways that our language reflects our neurology.
- Programming – because we can break free from the way that we have been programmed and choose to organise our ideas and actions the way we want.

Throughout this book, you will experience a range of NLP techniques you can follow to help you to move you forward faster and more easily, develop your coaching business and achieve the mindset for success.

The concept of modelling

I mentioned modelling in the last section. It is a term used in NLP, and it means to be able to replicate a desired skill, behaviour or state[1] in someone that can be taught to another person. Modelling essentially looks at the 'ability' of an individual with respect to a particular skill for the purpose of instilling similar behavioural patterns in oneself and others.

Modelling is an activity that children do well. During their personal development, they model the people around them. This includes both the negative and the positive characteristics of their parents, their peers, and their carers.

Modelling, in the frame of this project, was to model coaches who run a successful business. This consisted mainly of face-to-face interviews with 10 coaches. Through a series of questions and observations of their external and internal behaviours, my role was to elicit:

- Criteria specific to the skill of coaching and business success from their own perspective.
- Identify what motivates them and what is important to them.
- Understand what internal and external processes and behavioural patterns they use which enables them to be an excellent coach and business owner.

These criteria then allowed me to define what is actually required to run a successful coaching business and how I can teach these methods to people like you.

10 steps to transform your coaching practice

In this book, I will share with you the secrets of 10 successful coaches through modelling their success strategies. I also had the pleasure of interviewing Supercoach Michael Neill,

1 State refers to a person's emotional, physiological or psychological condition.

who is one of the world's best-known and most successful coaches. His success strategies and insights are also featured in this book.

In the next chapter I will outline the biographies of these coaches and successful business owners and the criteria I used to choose these models. I will then take you through the 10 steps for you to achieve success in your coaching business. I would advise you to read the book chapter by chapter, as each step builds upon the previous step and without it you will be missing an important piece of the jigsaw.

Undertake the activities suggested as I talk you through the process and also take some time to learn, reflect and, most importantly ... take action.

What are the 10 steps?

The 10 steps that we are following in this book are:

Step 1 – Create a values-based business
When you understand your values, it allows you to run a business based on your ideals and with a sense of true purpose.

Step 2 – Develop unstoppable self-belief
If you have an unstoppable self-belief, you can conquer the challenges you face with ease and bounce back from setbacks.

Step 3 – Become a business person
When you learn the skills to become a business person it allows you to create and develop the business you desire.

Step 4 – Develop your marketing skills
When you know what marketing strategies work for you, you can take action straight away to propel your business success.

Step 5 – Develop your networks
Building relationships is essential to running a coaching

business, and your networks will give you momentum to achieve success.

Step 6 – Be an expert in your field
The subject of niching is contentious, so learn how expertise can help you to achieve your business success.

Step 7 – Start with the end in mind
Having a vision for your business will enable you to get what you want, and ensure that every step you take is in the right direction.

Step 8 – Become work in progress
Through your ongoing development and learning you will continue to develop every day to achieve your personal and business success.

Step 9 – Develop a winning mindset
When you have a winning mindset, you can put your mind to anything and achieve success.

Step 10 – Learn from the experts
Take some time to learn from the successful coaches and find out how you can develop your own personal success story.

One last thing – what is success?

Finally, before I take you to the next stage and introduce you to my models, I would like to quickly define success.

For me, success is not just having knowledge about how to coach; it's having knowledge about how a business runs, and how to make it successful. It's not just the technical knowledge about product or service; it's about running a business and being able to do that side of things well. The mindset is the characteristics that make someone succeed.

What does success mean to you?

Chapter 2 – Introducing the models

When I started my modelling project, I chose to interview people who run successful coaching businesses, or incorporate coaching into their business model. All of the people profiled in this book gave up their time for me to interview them and have allowed me to share with you their innermost thoughts and strategies.

The people I modelled and interviewed at length were people who had achieved at least two of the following:

- Mastered coaching to the extent they are able to instil it in others.
- Run a business that is successful in that it meets their goals, values and beliefs.
- Have reached the pinnacle of their career and are happy with themselves, know what they are achieving through recognition on a consistent basis through media, press or other feedback such as courses, seminars or workshops.
- Have presented and spoken to large audiences, trained, authored books and/or articles.

I chose models who have inspired me, who have been recommended to me by people I trust, and who I respect for their knowledge and expertise. It has been a great experience to learn from these experts and I thank them for their time and support. For contact details, please go to 'Further resources'.

Allison Marlowe, Women's Business Coach

Allison Marlowe has a 'Make It Happen' attitude and works as a successful business coach and mentor with aspiring and established womenpreneurs. She is passionate about connecting women in business and is the founder of Hampshire Winning Women networking group and more recently the Hampshire Winning Women Business Awards.

Her views and opinions are often sought and she regularly contributes to local and national media. She lives by the sea in the South of England with her husband and her youngest three children.

Blaire Palmer, Executive Coach

Blaire Palmer was one of the first professional certified coaches in the UK and is one of the leading executive coaches in her field. Previously a top news producer for the BBC, she produced the corporation's flagship Radio 4 news programme 'Today' and the classic daily magazine 'Woman's Hour', working alongside some of the top presenters in the UK and helping to shape the news and current affairs agenda during that period.

Since leaving the BBC a decade ago, Blaire has gained a reputation for creating transformational results whether she is working with leaders one-to-one or with groups of executives or teams.

She is Managing Director and consultant with Taming Tigers Ltd, and a consultant with Cirrus Partners. She is the author of three books: *The Hyper-Creative Personality* (New Holland, 2007), *The Recipe for Success* (A & C Black, 2009) and *What's Wrong with Work?* (John Wiley & Sons, 2010). In addition she is a regular guest on Jeremy Vine's Radio 2 programme and writes a monthly column for Healthy magazine and HR Zone.

Dawn Breslin, Consciously Female Coach

Dawn Breslin is a bestselling author, radio broadcaster and motivational speaker. She is one of the UK's leading life transformational coaches and has been featured extensively on TV and in the media worldwide.

She is the author of *The Power Book: A 7-Step Life Makeover* (Hay House UK, 2005) and *Dawn Breslin's Guide to Superconfidence* (Hay House UK, 2006).

She is an expert in gently nurturing and empowering people to achieve a deep sense of joy and fulfilment in the lives that they live. Her vision is to show us how to dance with life and to recognise and celebrate the magic that exists in each and every moment that we breathe!

Duncan Brodie, Leadership Coach

Duncan Brodie is the Director of Goals and Achievements. Following twenty-five rewarding and successful years in the accountancy profession, managing and leading teams in a range of major organisations including PricewaterhouseCoopers, Ernst & Young, TSB (now Lloyds TSB) and the NHS, he decided it was time for a change. After working with a brilliant career coach he realised that what he really valued was helping others to achieve success.

Having climbed the career ladder from Accounts Clerk to Finance Director, he understands first-hand the challenges of managing and leading, particularly for those making the transition from highly technical roles. Helping those technically brilliant people to become brilliant managers and leaders and realise their true potential is what really motivates Duncan. In working with his clients his focus is on providing practical learning and development opportunities that raise performance and achievement levels.

Gladeana McMahon, Personal Development and Transformational Coach

Gladeana McMahon is considered one of the leading personal development and transformational coaches in the UK who combines academic rigour with down-to-earth communication skills. She holds a range of qualifications and is accredited by the British Association for Counselling and Psychotherapy, Association of Rational Emotive Behaviour Practitioners and the British Association for Behavioural and Cognitive Psychotherapies as both a therapist and coach.

She helped found the Association for Coaching (AC) for which she holds the positions of Fellow and Chair of the AC UK. She is also a Fellow of the British Association for Counselling and Psychotherapy, Institute of Management Studies and Royal Society of Arts. An innovator, Gladeana is one of the UK founders of Cognitive Behavioural Coaching and is an internationally published author with some sixteen books of a popular and academic nature on coaching and counselling to her name.

She has presented a range of coaching programmes and was listed as one of the UK's Top Ten Coaches by both The Independent and The Observer. She coaches CEOs and those at director level as well as politicians and those in the media to master the psychological complexities of 21st century corporate life.

Hannah McNamara, Marketing Coach

Hannah McNamara is a successful author and a qualified coach. With fifteen years' experience in sales and marketing, she now runs *Marketing Help for Coaches,* providing support and advice for those looking to start or build their own coaching practice. She frequently speaks at business exhibitions and events, and writes for various professional journals.

Hannah is a member of the International Coach Federation and the Chartered Institute of Marketing. She has experience with national and international organisations working on both the client-side and agency-side of marketing. She is the author of *Niche Marketing for Coaches* (Thorogood, 2007), which is sold worldwide.

Her own coaching practice specialises in career advancement, leadership and management. In 2006 she established the SME Academy with serial entrepreneur Patrick White and together they deliver the Business Growth Course, which has a proven record of transforming businesses.

Marian Way, Clean Language Coach

Marian started her career as a maths teacher and later worked for Weight Watchers as a group facilitator, a trainer, and finally as Programme Development Manager of Weight Watchers UK, where she and a colleague developed the POINTS diet. She later worked as a consultant to the organisation in the UK and the USA.

A skilled facilitator and trainer, Marian has developed and delivered training programmes which have benefited thousands of people across the world. She has personally delivered training in England, Northern Ireland, the USA, Spain and Russia. She also works with individuals and groups to enable them to achieve their goals. She is an NLP Master Practitioner and Trainer who specialises in applications based on *Clean Language*, which involves paying exquisite attention to people and the language they use to express their ideas.

Steve Marriott, Success Coach

Steve became one of the UK's leading success coaches following a highly successful career as a Learning & Development Manager in leisure and retail. Blending precise observation and insight with the very best developments in neuro-science, Steve works with people from all sectors to radically transform the way they bring success into all aspects of their work and home lives.

Steve is a pioneer in taking coaching to a new level, both in terms of the profound impact he has on those he coaches, and in the way he develops coaching capability inside organisations. His article *The New Coaches* and coaching support cards *Beyond Question*, are creating a revolution within the coaching community to move away from process driven interventions and put you at the heart of everything to deliver life-changing results in minutes.

Alongside his work in success coaching, Steve helps busy leaders to revolutionise the way they design and deliver presentations. Working with all experience levels and abilities, Steve has helped his clients create new approaches to presenting, from mastering instant confidence to going script-free to television presenting and keynote speeches. Steve's recent work has enabled him to observe and model many of today's best presenters to identify and replicate the micro differences between the great and the world-class.

Steve is proud to work in partnership with ASOS, ADT Tyco, Bourne Leisure, BSkyB, Centerparcs, Continuum Group, EDF Energy, Farnborough International, Halfords, Merlin Entertainments, Microchip, Sesame and Unum.

Suparna Dhar, Parent Coach, Trainer and Facilitator

After an extensive career in Human Resources, Suparna Dhar qualified as a Life Coach and launched her practice Life's Canvas based in Ruislip, Middlesex. Her practice concentrates on empowering parents and carers to gain focus, direction and confidence to improve their parenting skills to help them bring up engaged children through one-to-one coaching and bespoke workshops, based on the aims of *Every Child Matters*.

With vast experience working with clients such as The London Borough of Ealing, The London Borough of Hillingdon, Homestart–Ealing, Contact a Family, The JGA Group, Women's Refuges and Children's Centres, she has provided a wide range of bespoke workshops to meet the needs of the individual settings.

Her areas of expertise when working with the long-term unemployed include how to choose a new career, carrying out an effective job search, designing a powerful CV and improving interview techniques. She has also delivered Learning Skills Council and The Department of Work and Pensions funded programmes such as Skills Coaching and Skills4jobs which has targeted specific unemployed groups such as women returners and ex-offenders. She writes articles for on-line directories such as The Asian Business Community, is a proficient public speaker at schools on motivation and entrepreneurs and is a CIPD mentor.

Suzy Greaves, Big Leap Coach

Suzy Greaves is the UK's leading self development expert, author and journalist – named as 'one of the top ten gurus in the UK' by the Daily Mail.

Author of *Making The Big Leap* (New Holland Publishers, 2004), voted one of the top ten life-changing books by The Independent on Sunday, Suzy is a media columnist and celebrity coach and Managing Director of The Big Leap Coaching Company, which specialises in career change. *The Big Peace* (Hay House UK) was published in 2009 and named as 'the ultimate guide to contentment' by The Daily Express.

Michael Neill, Success Coach

As well as modelling these amazing coaches, I also had the opportunity to interview the American coach, Michael Neill.

Michael Neill is an internationally renowned success

coach and the best-selling author of *You Can Have What You Want*, *Feel Happy Now!* (Hay House, 2009) and the *Effortless Success* audio program (Hay House, 2008). He has spent the past twenty years as a coach, adviser, friend, mentor and creative spark plug to celebrities, CEOs, royalty, and people who want to get more out of their lives. His books have been translated into ten languages, and his public talks and seminars have been well received at the United Nations and on five continents around the world.

He hosts a weekly talk show on HayHouseRadio.com, and his newest book, *Supercoach: 10 Secrets to Transform Anyone's Life* was released by Hay House in 2010.

Chapter 3 –
Step 1 Create a values-based business

'Values are not just words; values are what we live by. They're about the causes we champion and the people we fight for.' – Senator John Kerry

What are your values?

Values are the things that are important to us. They are the basis on which many of our decisions are made, and affect our thoughts and actions.

Values provide the norms which guide our behaviour. They determine our attitudes towards what is right or wrong, and they provide us with moral principles which are used to rationalise any action.

Many people leave their job because it no longer meets their values. Your values contribute towards how satisfied you are at work. They can motivate you to do a job well and contribute towards what makes a job exciting and fun. So when you are creating your coaching business it makes sense to develop a business that meets your values and one that you are passionate about.

In your business, your values are those which are going to give you purpose to do what you do. As the effort, commitment and motivation that a person brings to a job or business are usually in direct proportion to the values they perceive in it, it is essential that your values are reflected in the business that you create.

You may have personal values, and those business owners

who are successful ensure that these values are reflected in the way they run their business. If your values are not congruent, your business is less likely to be successful.

Your values will drive your behaviour so wouldn't it help to have an idea of your values to ensure that these are reflected in your coaching business?

Everything you do is to fulfil your values, and to do this you either move away from what you don't want or move towards what you do want. These are called 'away from' or 'towards' values.

To put it simply, 'away from' values are those things that we want to move away from, such as pain in our lives. For example, a value may be 'not to be in poverty'. Conversely a 'towards' value is one that moves us towards pleasure, and an example of a 'towards' value may be around 'generating profit or income'.

Or as Dr Wyatt Woodsmall says: "Values are those things that we move toward or away from. They either attract us or repel us. They are what we are willing to invest time, energy and resources to achieve or avoid. All human decisions are based on values, which are usually outside of conscious awareness. Values are the basis of the criteria on which all decisions are made."

Few people are clearly aware of their own values, or perhaps they have worked on them in the past, but have not updated their values as their life develops and evolves.

If you know your values, you can:

- Be more in control of your actions and your emotions.
- Make better decisions, since you have greater awareness of what is truly important to you.
- Recognise what you need to do to feel good.
- Find lots of different ways of fulfilling them, rather than doing the same old things as before.

So before I tell you how you can clearly identify your own personal values, what are the values of my models?

Values present in successful coaching businesses

'Values are like a compass that directs your life.' – Anthony Robbins

All of the models interviewed for this project had a clear idea of their values and how these values were translated into their business. They all had a clear belief that to run their businesses successfully, their personal and business values had to be congruent. Many of the models stated that one of the reasons that they set up their business was to allow them to live a life they enjoy and to help others to do the same.

Interestingly, although all of my models run diverse coaching businesses with different business criteria, they had some values in common.

These are some of the values that were present:

- Being in touch with their values, feelings and desires
- Being authentic
- Integrity and honesty
- Having commitment to a course of action or another person
- Having passion about what they do
- Making a difference in other people's lives
- Being professional.

As a NLP Master Practitioner, I observed the language of my models when they talked about their values. They were mainly focused towards what they want rather than away from what they don't want. They demonstrated energy and positivity towards their passions.

Being in touch with their values, feelings and desires

When someone creates a business based around their values, they know the reasons why their business is important and how they can reflect this in their business model. Although not a value on its own, this statement is true for many of the models I interviewed for this book.

In our interview, Women's Business Coach, Allison Marlowe told me that she never had the intention of becoming self-employed. She was passionate about her previous career in primary and further education, but when she had children it became quite stressful. She started to realise that there was more to life than travelling to and from work and managing her team. During our interview, Allison recalled a situation at work:

"When I had my fourth child I went back to work when she was six weeks old. She was in a baby seat and I was trying to breastfeed her and type with one hand and I can remember sitting there and thinking that 'I can't do this.' I thought I was the only person at the college that could do those specific things but I persevered a little bit longer, as I didn't know then what I know now."

Like many people who become coaches, she had the opportunity to be coached and she recalled realising that when she was in this situation, she thought 'I could do this.' Within a month she had signed up to do the coaching training. She then made the decision that she was not going back to work.

Then, following this realisation, Allison told me that her number one value is her family. "Family comes first – always," she said. "If anything was to happen, God forbid, touch wood, to any of my children or my husband or anything then I would drop everything and this is one of the reasons I set up my business because I wanted it to fit my lifestyle very much."

Gladeana McMahon made this comment: "If you don't think your business is fun, don't do it."

Being authentic

There are a couple of values here which are intertwined. Under the umbrella term 'authenticity', it can be defined by 'being true to oneself' and 'being both genuine and real'.

The value of authenticity is championed by Gladeana McMahon. "Being authentic is what you see is what you get," she said. "If I'm not authentic, it won't work, but you also have to be a chameleon when it is appropriate. Success is as much about who you are as what you do."

Suzy Greaves told me that her business is based around trust. "It's about trust, people trusting you and who you are and that you're authentic and real, not doing things just to get business."

Integrity and honesty

Integrity and honesty are two other values that were mentioned by many of the models I interviewed for this project. This includes integrity and honesty in what they do and also in relation to the way they work with other people.

Marian Way: "My biggest value is to be a clean business where people matter more than the process. It is important that people are heard, listened to, and I'd rather not sell something to somebody if it isn't right for them, right now."

Steve Marriott: "Integrity means that I will always go with the truth, as uncomfortable as it may be. If I believe that someone's logic is totally flawed or I believe I know the reason they aren't getting what they want, I will tell them that rather than let them have false hopes."

Dawn Breslin: "Everything I do is based around honesty, truth, integrity, pureness, just a lightless about life. I want to be on track spiritually, and offer the truth. That is who I am and in a work sense, I follow through, I am true to my word, I work hard and I will get results."

Gladeana McMahon: "There is integrity also in terms of charging money. I have no qualms about charging money. I've learnt how to do it because everybody tends to feel uncomfortable at first. I know that as long as I'm adding value, I have no qualms about charging."

Having commitment to a course of action or another person

Commitment to a course of action and tenacity are values that came out in all of my models. They focus on making things happen and working with other people to do this. When I asked Hannah McNamara about her values, she told me that she was client-focused, which links in with this value. "I think within the client-focus value there is customer service," she said. "It's about finding a way to do things for a client when you are working with them. I'm not going, 'Oh, I've got this lovely new coaching technique I want to use.' I'm just going with what they need at that time. Sometimes people get too hung up on them and their own skills when they are trying to coach some people and they forget that it's about the client.

"It's actually got nothing to do with you and your abilities; it's what that client needs at that given time. Sometimes they need to be coached, sometimes they need to be taught, and sometimes they just need to offload. And they don't want someone saying, 'So what are you going to do about it?' They just want to hear 'Oh God, that sounds awful.'"

Allison Marlowe: "I think that when you believe in something strongly, it is important to see it through. I think this stems from my mother who would start something but would never finish it. For me it has been important from a young age, whatever I started, I had to complete. At junior school, the motto was 'nil desperandum' – never despair, never give up, and it really struck a chord. I do get a lot of satisfaction now from seeing things through, but they need to be the things *I* choose to see through."

Having passion about what they do

All of my models are passionate about what they do and in doing so have greater balance and fulfilment in their life.

They have the freedom to make choices and live their lives on their terms.

This came out when I was interviewing Suzy Greaves. "My business values are the same as my personal values – creativity, connection, and learning," she said. "I'm at my happiest always when I am creative, when I am writing. Coming up with ideas is something I do naturally and always have done. When I am living that value I'm really happy. Again something I've done naturally all my life is that I want to connect. I get really bored with small talk, I want to know what makes someone tick, how happy they are and I want to express how I feel and get that real proper connection."

Gladeana McMahon has been running her business for over twenty years, and shows obvious passion. When I asked her whether success is linked to her values, she replied: "Success is about being true to who you are. I think you have to know yourself; you have to know what matters to you. Of course life is about trade-offs; you can't have everything you would like, however nice that would be. But I think it is about your values and checking in with yourself as your values can change over time. I'm going to be fifty-six next year, and I've changed over the years. What I wanted and was passionate about at twenty-three is still me but there are differences. I often joke and say I suffer from 'have mouth, will travel', and I'm still the person who puts their hand up and says: 'Oh I'll have a go.' I've still got those traits because they are part of who I am. But at twenty-three, I was into saving the world; it was very important to go out there and be the best therapist I could. My passion is now around coaching and self-help and I'm not so into wanting to save everybody. Now it's about how important it is for people to enjoy their lives, really enjoy their lives ... My by-line is: 'when life gets in the way of living.'" She continued: "Enthusiasm is a personal trait that I will never lose. I will probably be the most enthusiastic corpse you will see in my box. In fact the theme tune on my mobile is 'always look on the bright side of life!'"

To concur with this value, Suparna Dhar told me that she needed a passion for coaching and a belief in the benefits of coaching. "Success means being the best coach I can be and leading a life that is in balance, in keeping with my values," she said.

Making a difference in other people's lives

I don't believe that you can run a successful coaching business unless you are committed to making a difference to other people's lives.

Linked closely to passion, this value came out with all of my models. This included Leadership Coach, Duncan Brodie, who said: "If you are somebody who is only looking at the three bars on the gaming machine and thinking about the money, you are never going to make it in this business. I think you have to have a bias towards caring about others and others' success. To me, if you haven't got that, you're never going to make it as a coaching business."

Allison Marlowe: "I feel passionate about what I believe and the people I work with and like to bring out the best in everyone. I also believe that we all encounter problems big and small and we all overcome personal challenges and for some they are much worse than others. And if I can help somebody in any little way, that brings me back to that place of being successful and satisfied."

Suparna Dhar told me about her business and her passions. "Life's Canvas is about empowering parents in order to bring up engaged children. Empowered parents have the confidence to make informed decisions, so they can bring up their children in the way they want to – in a positive way."

Gladeana McMahon: "Success is about a need to feel safe and secure, so finance is important but success is also about enjoying what I do. Success is also about being with other people and seeing them grow and develop, and having the satisfaction of having had some part in that, however small."

In addition, Steve made a very pertinent comment during our interview: "Bluntly speaking, if you are not going to be happy or find happiness, you are going to be fannying around on a rock in space for ninety years. In my background and during my upbringing, I have met and worked with so many people who have limited themselves and deferred their happiness. The people I work with challenge those rules and get on with it. So many people with encouragement and help can do so much with their lives."

Being professional

Professionalism is another value which is key to running a successful coaching business.

Duncan Brodie: "Professionalism for me is about being ethical, business-like in your dealings, thinking about your reputation and protecting that and getting known as somebody who persistently gives good stuff. It is about consistency, actually."

Hannah McNamara: "Professionalism is the phones getting answered and replying to emails where possible within a certain period of time. It is also about being well presented, articulate and not turning up to sign a contract for several thousands of pounds with a chewed pen!"

How to create a values-based business

'It's not hard to make decisions when you know what your values are.' – Roy Disney

As I mentioned earlier, many people leave an organisation because their personal values no longer match the corporate vision and values of the company. Therefore, isn't making sure there is a match between your personal and business values a great starting point when setting up your own business?

Suzy Greaves agreed with me. "I think we've all been in jobs that we've hated," she said. "When I first started out, after doing my degree, I ended up doing crappy jobs; selling photocopiers, selling coca cola machines, all sorts of things. Work is one of the most important things we spend our time on. It's where we spend so much of our energy; it's about the purpose that we are here. So I think it is so important that we love our jobs, we enjoy our jobs and we are doing the best with the skills that we've got. It's that thing of keep pushing yourself to do something new and fresh, and I think that's what gives me excitement; that's one of the great things about having your own business."

If you don't run a values-based business, you may face feeling overwhelmed, confused, have a lack of direction, lack of focus, have no clear action steps, or become out of balance.

When you have a business that meets your values, you have the energy to jump out of bed in the morning, to manage your clients' needs and to drive your business forward. It also gives you clarity and focus around the objectives of your business. This then enables you to create your personal vision and mission for your business based around what you want for your own success.

Brian Tracy in his popular CD set, Success Mastery Academy, says:

"Values are the core of who you are. All exceptional people know who they are. Who you are *is* your values. Who you are is your values organised by priority. Successful people are clear about what they believe in and stand for, and they don't compromise those values, there's no question.

"The interesting thing is when you know who you are and what you stand for it is quite easy to make decisions in your life. Because they are either in or they are out, it's very simple. Unsuccessful people are fuzzy, they are unclear, they are unsure. They will compromise their values if an advantage or possibility comes up; compromise it in favour of some advantage or possibility. But for you, it's not acceptable; your job is to be crystal clear about what you stand for and crystal clear in the order of your values."

Thank you to Brian Tracy for giving me permission to publish this quote. Here is a little more information about Brian:

Brian Tracy is the most listened to audio author on personal and business success in the world today. His fast-moving talks and seminars on leadership, sales, managerial effectiveness and business strategy are loaded with powerful, proven ideas and strategies that people can immediately apply to get better results in every area. For more information, please go to www.briantracy.com.

To create your own values-based business, the first step you need to take is to know your values or update the values that you think you have. Values are a subject that many coaches will cover during their coach training, but it is easy for these to get out of date during the journey of developing a business. That is why they need to be updated on a regular basis to ensure they reflect who you think you are.

Once you know your values, you can create a plan or vision for your business based around these values.

- If you value financial success, make sure your business plan reflects this aim.
- If you value time with your family, ensure your business allows you the right balance in your life.
- If you value enjoyment and happiness, create a business that you are passionate about.

NLP Values Elicitation exercise

The NLP values elicitation exercise is designed to help you to update and clarify your values. In doing this exercise you will identify what is important to you and be able to prioritise those that need to be present in your business.

Part 1: If possible, work with a partner, and then swap over once the entire exercise has been completed with the first person.

Ask your partner the following question: What is important to you about your coaching business?

Note down the answer word for word, making sure you use the person's own words or phrases. Do not change the wording. Once you have the answer, rephrase the question to: What else is important to you about your coaching business? Keep on asking the question until at least 10 values are listed below.

1.

2.

3.

4.

5.

6.

7.

8.

9.

10.

Part 2: Rank the values according to their level of importance. To do this read the list of values you have written down to your partner. Then ask your partner:

a) Are these your values? (if not repeat part 1)

b) Of the values you have mentioned to me, which is the most important to you?

Once you have ranked the number 1 value, you can continue to rank the others by going down the list using two questions below:

a) Assuming you have [list value(s) already chosen], is _____ (the next value on the list) or _____ (the value statement after that one) more important to you?

b) Assuming you have _____ (next value statement on the list) but you could not have _____ (the value statement after that one) would that be OK?

Part 3: Rewrite the values below according to their importance. Then swap roles.

1.

2.

3.

4.

5.

6.

7.

8.

9.

10.

Once you know and understand your values you can make sure that these are reflected in your life and your business. Are there any tweaks that you need to make right now?

_____

_____

Now that you understand your values, let's look at your beliefs and how these can affect your business.

Chapter 4 –
Step 2 Develop unstoppable self-belief

'Beliefs have the power to create and the power to destroy. Human beings have the awesome ability to take any experience of their lives and create a meaning that disempowers them or one that can literally save their lives.'
– Anthony Robbins

Although your values are an integral part of who you are and what your business stands for, knowing your values on their own is not enough to create a successful coaching business. The next step on your journey is to develop an unstoppable and unwavering self-belief. Although you may have covered this area during your coaching training, it is also important to take time to work on your own beliefs around your business and your personal and professional success.

What are beliefs?

A belief is:

1. The mental act, condition, or habit of placing trust or confidence in another.
2. Mental acceptance of, and conviction in, the truth of something.
3. Something believed or accepted as true.

Also, you could say that there are beliefs about beliefs:

- You can choose which beliefs you want.
- You can change your own beliefs.
- You can hold two contradictory beliefs at the same time.

Your beliefs will come out through the language you use (words, phrases, and metaphors), the physiology that you express, and the behaviour that you demonstrate.

What you believe in helps to create the reality that you experience. If you *feel* in a certain way, e.g. negative or frustrated, it does not mean you *are* a certain way, but this is related to the emotion that you feel at that particular time. But what you believe in does create the reality that you experience. The mind sorts information so that events are always matched to the established belief, and all other information is ignored.

A belief is associated with a particular state of mind and often acts as a filter, determining what a person pays attention to and includes information that is deleted, distorted or filtered. At any time in our lives, we have millions of bits of information coming into our minds through our five senses of sight, touch, sound, taste and smell, but only a small chunk of this information is consciously registered. Our values and beliefs contribute strongly to our personal map of the world that each of us has, which links to our own perception of our reality. This means that what is reality for you may not be the same for someone else.

We have each got a set of core beliefs that may or may not serve us well in our lives. Research suggests that as a child we were born with two fears – a fear of loud noises and a fear of falling. Yet as we grow older and become adults, we gain many more fears, beliefs and doubts that prevent us from fulfilling our potential. Many of the beliefs we have now are as a result of situations we faced as a younger person and our responses to those situations.

These stem from relationships with our parents or carers, our teachers, and our peer group.

Beliefs can limit your business

'I can't believe that!' said Alice.
'Can't you?' the Queen said in a pitying tone.
'Try again: draw a long deep breath, and shut your eyes.'

Alice laughed. 'There's no use trying,' she said, 'one can't believe impossible things.'

'I dare say you haven't had much practice,' said the Queen. 'When I was your age I always did it for half an hour a day. Why sometimes I've believed as many as six impossible things before breakfast.'

Through the Looking Glass by Lewis Carroll

What beliefs do you have that don't serve you well in your life or your business?

It doesn't take much to make us feel bad about ourselves which can then create a downward spiral. Then in many situations, it can become a self-fulfilling prophecy. If you believe that you can't do something, this will be ingrained in your subconscious, and then you will go about convincing yourself that it is true. For example, you may believe that you are not very good at networking with other business people, so when you go out to a networking event (if you actually do so at all) you will probably stand in a corner, not engage with other people, and fail to make a great impression. This evidence then reinforces your self-belief. OK, maybe this is an extreme example, but given the same information, someone with a strong self-belief will learn how to network with others, take time to develop and practise their perfect pitch and persevere to build up their networks with other people.

During our interview, Steve Marriott told me how he

sees beliefs as hindering people. "People are bought up with rules and inherit beliefs from other people," he said, "and are scared of breaking them. They create belief systems to support their behaviour and reinforce feelings that they are not worthy, which doesn't serve them. This may be a huge generalisation but most of these 'rules' have been learned from their parents or teachers, which cause a self-destructive pattern. All your parents really want is for you to be happy, but then, with the very best of intentions, they impose their map of the world on us."

So beliefs are those things that you believe are true (whether they are or not is a different matter). If you believe they are true, you will build up evidence to convince yourself, which will then drive your behaviour and how you react to the situation. In addition, your behaviour will drive other people's behaviour to reinforce your own belief. But I do have some good news for you! Your past doesn't have to equal your future. If you think about those of you who used to believe in the tooth fairy or Father Christmas, but don't anymore, you can soon change your beliefs.

But even the most experienced coaches have beliefs that don't serve them well in their business at times. But they are aware of these beliefs and take action to counter their effect on themselves and their business.

In our interview, Suzy Greaves referred to having a big and a small place. "What I want is that sense of feeling content, of being able to ride the roller coaster of life. Sometimes it is really crap, sometimes it's really fantastic." Going on to talk about the big and small place, she says: "A sense of being big is coming from your expanded self, coming from a sense of expansion, love, your best self rather than your small self, that which is fearful and competitive. You need to make decisions from your big self and to make the big leap it will be more successful if you come from the big place. But having said that we all go into the small place; we all have that place and it's accepting that is part of it. Always try to make decisions at least from your big place; that's what I am trying to do with my business."

I asked Suzy what she does to make sure she makes decisions from her big place. "I am very human and the first thing is about being aware and then making a definite choice not to go there and to go to a more expansive place." She went on to say, "I think it is also about being accepting. It's OK to be down and it is quite exhausting to be up all the time. I always thought there was a place called 'there' where I would be 'da-dah' all the time and that's not the case. We are human and have the same problems that other people have as well."

Similarly, Gladeana McMahon admits that she is a fallible human being and that at times she can be critical about herself. But she also told me that she no longer takes herself too seriously.

I asked Executive Coach, Blaire Palmer whether she has any beliefs that don't serve her well in her business. "I have had beliefs around being found out as a fraud, not believing that I'm a fraud, but thinking that other people will think I'm a fraud," she said. "Those have not been helpful at all. Sometimes I have to be quite conscious, even now, of getting myself in the right frame of mind to walk into a big meeting. But I've always found these people, once you've got to know them, are exactly the same as you."

Steve Marriott: "In the first couple of years there's always that 'Who am I to be successful?' and all of that kind of stuff. And it still does creep in every now and again." I asked him what he does if this takes place. "I slap myself internally," he said. "When I have what I call a 'wobble', what I envisage is a metaphor – like stepping into a pool of light. It soon goes away when I focus on it. When I'm at my best, I'm not even in the equation, I envisage all the energy radiating towards the person I am working with."

Duncan Brodie told me that it takes a strong self-belief to run a business, which I do agree is true. "If you haven't got the confidence to put yourself out there, if you are somebody who is going to get hurt when rejected, you are never going to get your business off the ground. You will get clients that don't work out, things you deliver that people don't like and you need to be able to bounce back. A lot of personal resilience is needed for that. Don't lose sight of what you've done and acknowledge these things."

Beliefs that can empower your business

'Whether you believe you can or you can't, you're probably right.' – Henry Ford

Beliefs don't have to limit your progression. There is nothing stopping you developing a set of empowering beliefs that will serve you well in your business. Empowering beliefs are ones that are outcome-focused, positive, and impact positively on how you feel about yourself.

We each run our own script inside our heads about how good we are or whether we can achieve something. If you make the beliefs you have positive, you will be even more successful. Your beliefs are up to you; it is your decision whether you believe you can or cannot do something. If you want to run a successful coaching business, the first belief that you need to have is to believe in yourself that you can do this. Once you have this determination and attitude, you will be sending a congruent message to your brain that you want to achieve your objectives and get results.

Hannah McNamara: "I think there needs to be a lot of self-belief that you can do it. And not allowing any doubt to get in your mind and not allowing any 'I don't know if I'm cut out for this kind of stuff,' because that's really poisonous ... I don't have time for those kinds of thoughts. They spread – you can't let them in. If you start to doubt yourself, you destroy everything. You can make a decision about what you're not best suited for and you can make a decision where something hasn't worked and change it."

Hannah's tip: "Give yourself a pep talk when you need one." If something has gone wrong, you can ask yourself what went wrong, what you can do about it, what you can change, what you can do differently. Often you will find that your own criticism isn't noticed by your client and is your own interpretation about your performance. If you want to find out how you can be a better coach, ask for feedback from your clients to improve even further.

I asked Gladeana McMahon about her beliefs around her business. "Do the right things and good things will happen," she said.

Dawn Breslin: "The difference between someone who is or is not successful is that total self-belief. That self-belief comes through getting feedback, not being frightened of criticism, learning from it. That starts to show you what is good about you. And if you are on track and you're doing what's right for you, you will be good at it. If you are doing what's wrong for you, you might not. So it's really important that you are aligned and in the right place. When you go into the work you go into flow; you go into the work and you feel excited. It feels fairly effortless. If you're going into the work and it's a struggle, you hate it and you wobble about it. Is it actually right or does it need to be adjusted ever so slightly? We excel where we feel comfortable, we feel passionate, and we feel aligned."

Suzy Greaves: "Sometimes I get scared – I don't know what I can do. Am I good enough? I still have the whole old patterns running in my head but it's OK as I'll do it anyway. So it's not that I don't feel fear, it's that I overcome it. But when I've done it, I feel so proud of myself and feel very excited and passionate again."

Many of us have self-talk, or an inner dialogue that can easily hold us back, especially when we are in a situation which is unfamiliar or scary. Self-talk is a combination of inner thoughts and mental chatter that affect our feelings and emotions. It includes what you say to yourself and how you say it. It may be negative, critical, or chastising, or it can be positive, empowering or calming.

Allison Marlowe had this to say about her self-talk: "The majority of the time the self-talk is positive and obviously depends on what's occurring; I'm only human – I do have a negative as well. But what I have learnt very much is to listen to that side of self-talking and I can actually say: 'No, that's not helpful,' 'That's not helping you,' or 'That's not a belief that you have any more.' Sometimes you can catch yourself quite quickly but other times you might experience something and you don't realise until afterwards that you have fallen back into old habits, but generally it's very positive. I would say there is a tendency to push myself in that self-talk: 'You have done that once before, so you can do it again.' Those are the kinds of comments that I find myself hearing."

So with that in mind, make sure that your self-talk is positive, empowering and affirming.

Develop an unstoppable self-belief

'The thing always happens that you really believe in; and the belief in a thing makes it happen.' – Frank Lloyd Wright

Many entrepreneurs in history and in the present day have been turned down hundreds of times in their journey to develop a business. From Thomas Eddison, Colonel Sanders to Sir Richard Branson and one of the Dragons, Duncan Bannatyne, they have overcome what seems like unmistakeable odds to achieve their dreams. One of the qualities of many successful entrepreneurs and business owners is that they make decisions and they take action.

Big Leap Coach, Suzy Greaves told me that she has to have courage and be brave. She says: "People ask me why big leapers are successful and I say it's because we're still scared but we do it anyway. The feeling when you're not being brave is horrible, it's like indecisive, not knowing. I suppose I ask the question what is the brave thing to do here? If I was brave what would I do? What's the worst that can happen?"

Executive Coach, Blaire Palmer: "Success takes bravery, courage or something. You do things that frighten you; you feel the fear and do it anyway. And in time these things don't frighten you anymore, and new things frighten you as you've gone one layer deeper than you had before. If you don't like that, if what you imagined when you wanted to be a coach was sitting at home waiting for the phone to ring, and anything beyond that frightens you, frightens you in a way that you are not willing to address, then you are not going to be able to make a go of it."

When you do decide to be brave, decide what you want to achieve and go do it. Many athletes like to visualise their success, so take a step back and visualise yourself being successful at whatever is holding you back. See yourself in the situation in technicolour, what you will see, hear and feel. See it going well, hear the positive comments that people will say about you and feel how you will feel once the situation has been successful. If you just jump into the situation and think, 'Oh, it's not going to work,' what do you think will happen then?

Take some time to prepare for the situation you are facing. If you are going to a networking event, prepare your perfect pitch. Who do you want to meet and what are you going to say? Then take action to reinforce your new positive beliefs.

If you do want to create a new set of empowering beliefs you could also try developing some affirmations that will support you to do this.

An affirmation is about creating a word or phrase that you read out loud every day that you can believe is true. Developing your own set of powerful and positive affirmations can help you to positively develop your business and your own belief in yourself that you will be successful.

It is not always easy to develop an unstoppable self-belief, especially if you feel that your business is not going to plan, you are finding some aspects hard or you have been turned down by a potential client. But take some solace from Women's Business Coach, Allison Marlowe, who states: "I believe that nothing lasts forever, there is a belief for me that one door closes and another one opens. Nothing is ever final; there is always something else that might be something different, something new, something fresh. Sometimes doors have to close to let something new in, like decluttering your office – you have to make space for new files."

Executive Coach, Blaire Palmer continued: "To get in the right frame of mind comes from experience. Coaching people one-to-one is a huge advantage as you get to see the squishy insides of those very high-up people. If these people are like that, probably everyone is like that. They might seem 'crunchy' on the outside, but most of us have fears and all of that on the inside. 'Fraud syndrome' is found the world over. If there is a name for it, a lot of people must be feeling it. The privilege of seeing those squishy insides of people is very reassuring. You have to trust you come across better than you think. I've had good feedback even when I've not been feeling 100%."

NLP neurological levels exercise

The neurological levels model was designed by Robert Dilts[2] and inspired by the work of Gregory Bateson. It is designed to help you to remove blocks and to create a change which will last to ensure you are aligned to your business and personal goals. Although it relates to more than just changing your beliefs, it is a great exercise to ensure that you develop your business in line with your purpose, values, beliefs and capabilities.

According to Dilts, the process of learning and change takes place at different levels in the mind. There are six levels to the exercise, and each one influences other levels in the hierarchy. These levels are:

2. Thank you to Robert Dilts for allowing me to include this exercise in my book. Go to www.nlpu.com for further information on his work.

- Environment – where and when something occurs; for example, you may believe that one location gives you great opportunities where another constrains you.
- Behaviour – what specific behaviours support or do not support you.
- Capabilities – how you do things, the strategies you use consciously and unconsciously.
- Beliefs and values – consider why your values (what is important to you) and your beliefs (what you believe to be true) impact on your response to situations.
- Identity – who you believe you are, made up of your core values and beliefs, your purpose and mission.
- Vision – this highest level is associated with a sense of connection with a higher purpose.

This exercise can be done either in a linear fashion or spatially. If you choose to do this exercise spatially, start by writing down each of the six different levels on to separate A4 sheets of paper and laying them on the floor in the following order: environment, behaviour, capabilities, beliefs and values, identity, and vision. Then working with a partner, stand on the piece of paper named 'environment'. Your partner can then ask you the questions below and record your responses. Then move on to the next piece of paper until you conclude with 'vision'.

Environment – Where? When?
Ask yourself, where are my external constraints and opportunities? What are they?

Behaviour – What?
Ask yourself, what specific behaviours do I have that support me and what behaviours do not support me? (actions and reactions)

Capabilities – How?
Ask yourself, what strategies and states do I currently have available? (maps and plans)

Beliefs and Values – Why?
Ask yourself, what motivates me? What do I believe about myself/others? (values and meanings)

Identity – Who am I?
Ask yourself, what is my mission?

Vision – What else? Who else?
Ask yourself, what is my purpose?

Once you have completed this exercise, swap over and take your partner through the exercise too.

Make a note of what you have learnt below.

_____
_____
_____
_____
_____
_____
_____
_____

Once you understand your beliefs and the real purpose of why you have set up your coaching business and what you want to achieve, it makes it easier to align your business to your values. Once you start to understand what, if anything, is holding you back, it allows you to take the next steps and become a business person as well as a coach.

Chapter 5 –
Step 3 Become a business person

'To succeed in business, to reach the top, an individual must know all it is possible to know about that business.' – J P Getty

The mistake that many coaches make when they start out in business is that they expect clients to come to them without them taking any action. They train as a coach, but don't develop the mindset that they are actually running a business and need all the knowledge and expertise that comes with this.

That's not to say that some of the most successful coaches didn't start off that way, but they quickly realised that they had to develop the business skills to get ahead.

There are various skills required of a business person. To list just a few, these include:

- Having a plan for the business, a vision to create a successful business and also a passion for the business you are creating
- Knowing your clients and what they are seeking
- Networking skills and the ability to make connections
- Influencing and persuasion skills
- Sales and marketing skills
- The ability to manage the financial side of the business
- Productivity and motivation
- The knowledge and skills to be great at what you do.

Women's business coach, Allison Marlowe: "When I initially set up, I set up as a life coach and I decided to call my business Pace of Life Coaching. I'd had some fantastic training, and a very little bit on marketing yourself. I honestly believed that I was going to go home, build my website and I was going to go out there and people were going to phone me up. And I was going to go to networking events and people were going to say, 'Of course I want you to help me sort out all my life's problems.' It was really naïve, but at the time, I just didn't know."

Through her own personal development and by supporting her clients, initially as a parent coach and most recently as a Women's Business Coach, Allison now teaches business and marketing skills to her clients. Although she has experienced lack of knowledge herself in the past, she has learnt the skills to make her business a success. She now works with experts to help her to stand out from the crowd. This enables her to help other business women not to make the same mistakes and to achieve their goals much quicker and more successfully than they could do on their own.

My story

'Every day do something that will inch you closer to a better tomorrow.' – Doug Firebaugh

I admit I went through the same experience myself. After experiencing coaching to help me to refocus my stuck career, I trained to become a coach myself. I trained with one of the UK's leading coaching organisations in 2006, and when I qualified in the November, I did not have a clue about how to run a business. I set up my business, Self Discovery Coaching, but like many new coaches, I expected clients to come to me as I knew I had a great service to offer to them.

When I started, I set up my own website, and got some

business cards printed and vaguely niched myself as a life coach for women. I knew that one of the things I needed to do was to start networking. To be honest, my first taste of networking was a bit of a disaster and to top it all, after niching as a women's life coach, it was with a group of men!

I did find it hard at the beginning because of my mindset. Clients were not forthcoming at the start so I took the sensible option of keeping my full time job whilst developing my business during evenings and weekends. But even so, I didn't give up. I developed my coaching skills by offering pro bono coaching to get some more testimonials and case studies.

From a marketing point of view, like many coaches and small business owners, I made the mistake of getting leaflets printed before I had clearly decided what I had to offer to my clients. However, word of mouth started to work for me and eventually clients started trickling in and my business began to grow. But ultimately, I had my own coach mentor who was, and continues to be, invaluable. She motivates me, supports me and gives me strategies that work.

I also continued my own development through NLP and attended other short courses, as well as reading tons of business books. I got support. I had an accountant from day one. When I was ready, I employed a Virtual Assistant to help me, as well as a PR and Marketing expert and web designer. Then eventually I learnt how to shift my mindset from being a coach to being a business woman and developed some great relationships with like-minded business people. I then clarified my niche, developed my business vision and plan, played to my strengths and developed stretching goals. Although it took just over three years, it was an incredible journey (and still is!), but I wish I could have learnt from other successful coaches sooner!

What the coaching companies don't tell you

'Don't limit yourself. Many people limit themselves to what they think they can do. You can go as far as your mind lets you. What you believe, remember, you can achieve.'
– Mary Kay Ash

I am not going to say anything detrimental about any coaching training companies. My experience with one of the UK's leading coaching training companies was that the training was fantastic; the trainers were knowledgeable and supportive. But what the coaching training companies don't give you are many of the skills you need to run a business or indeed, make you aware of the need to have a 'business mindset'.

Many of them don't teach you the business skills, the marketing skills, or prepare you in how to network or to get new clients. But that can be the same for other training companies too. I recently worked with a nutritionist who was also going through a similar experience following her training. Although she was trained to be a nutritionist, she did not have the knowledge and expertise to run a successful business and was learning the skills along her journey.

There are some alarming statistics. "The stats are awful," said Supercoach, Michael Neill. "One study showed that only 20% of coaches are earning as much as 20,000 USD a year. I think this is to do with the way coach training is sold and marketed. You have so many people who are theoretically in the profession but don't have the first bit of knowledge or support to actually create a successful coaching business."

"I think you can learn the business skills," Michael continued. "You don't have to have them before you start. But if you don't at least recognise that there is a business element to running a coaching business, then you're missing something kind of fundamental."

Michael told me that this is why he now works with

coaches, through his Supercoach Academy, to help them to become more successful.

Steve Marriott echoed Michael's comments: "Coaching has a bad press in the UK. They push people through the GROW model or some other process, but it doesn't respect the person as an individual. They may have an idea of their goal, but it's often not that clear-cut or well defined. The coach may not have the skills or confidence to go off-piste and find the best intervention for that person at that time. From my experience some people go on an NLP workshop or coaching course, get a load of tools and 'inflict' them on people and charge them money for it. I believe that is worse in the short and long term for the client; the results are less about them and more about the coach."

The perception that many people get is a 'get rich quick' mentality as you can charge a substantial amount to clients, but they don't mention how much time it will take to network and market yourself to get these clients. That's not to say that you can't run a successful and profitable business, but that it takes focus and perseverance to make it work and to add value to the clients too.

People who are attracted to coaching tend to be caring individuals who want to make a difference to other people's lives.

Marketing Coach, Hannah McNamara: "I did some research recently among coaches and the number one reason for becoming a coach was to make a difference. And I think that's what most people really want to do. For some people it's making a difference by helping someone to discover who they are. For me it's about making a difference in their professional and work life and so helping them. For example, I had a client recently who was passed over for promotion time and time again and since we have been doing the work together, she's nailed that promotion to director. She's really pleased and that is a success, whether or not I make any money out of it."

Dawn Breslin: "It's women getting together talking about

life and how to redirect their life. But a big part of it is educational, it's not just 'Let's do the GROW model and set some goals.' It's putting in a really strong foundation of self-esteem, self confidence and a foundation of spiritual values that will sustain people through the really tough times, so that they can feel a sense of calm and peace in their lives. If you can have that and achieve a sense of purpose, to me you've cracked it. You've got what is awesome; you get up and you are doing what you love and you feel you can manage life. That's great! By default they set their own goals and find their direction."

Business skills

No matter what your product is, you are ultimately in the education business. Your customers need to be constantly educated about the many advantages of doing business with you, trained to use your products more effectively, and taught how to make never-ending improvement in their lives.' – Robert G Allen

In our interview, this is what marketing expert, Hannah McNamara, said about running a successful business: "It takes some business sense, and you don't have to have that before you start but you have got to be willing to learn it. It's no good entering a coaching career thinking you are changing your career because you're not. A career is about being employed and somebody else going out and bringing the money in and paying you. It's not about being employed; it's about having a business. You have to take responsibility for that, and you have to take responsibility for doing things that feel uncomfortable and that you don't enjoy doing. I think too often people say, 'If it doesn't feel right, it can't be the right path for me.' Well, doing a spreadsheet might not feel nice, but if you need to have that in order to get some money from the bank to get your business off the ground, then you are going to have to do it."

"Have a plan," says Hannah. "Don't say the universe will sort it all out or destiny will take a hand and if I am meant to be successful in this then someone will appear on my doorstep with a basketful of cash. You've got to have a plan. Even if it's on the back of an envelope, you've got to know where you are going and what you're going to do to get there. It doesn't have to be something big; it can be a one-pager that's stuck on your wall or something. It could be a mind map. Within having a business plan is knowing your market, knowing your product, and knowing your pricing, what you are going to do with your product; that's all in the plan."

When I asked Gladeana McMahon what it takes to run a successful business, she replied: "It takes drive, enthusiasm, determination, self-discipline, knowledge and business knowledge. You may only be one person but you still need to know how to make sure you are financially sound and how to do book-keeping and administration, as well as knowing enough about marketing. I would say that a self-employed person is like a GP, in that if you think about a GP, they can turn their hand to most things in terms of diagnosis, understanding, and then refer to a consultant when it gets above a certain level."

So you don't have to have business skills to create your coaching business, but you need to learn them pretty quickly. In the early days, you won't just be a coach; you may be the accountant, secretary, web designer, sales person, marketer and copywriter. Although you may be able to afford to get help and support in time, this may not be possible straight away.

Duncan Brodie: "I got trained, set up my business, but like many people I realised that I didn't know much about running a business. When you are working in a big organisation with all the infrastructure, it is dead easy. You start off running and you have a business and suddenly you realise ... How do I get a domain name? How do you get a website? How does all that work? How do I stream things in audio? How do I deal with that stuff? I really didn't know." But like all of the successful coaches, it didn't take Duncan long to learn what to do.

Marian Way came across the same problem. "I spent a lot of time fiddling around with websites, as I didn't know what to do to start with," she said. "It took me a while to realise that it's not about sitting on your backside writing stuff on websites, it's about going out there, talking to people and networking."

What many people find during the early stages is that they don't know where to start; they don't have a clear business model or idea of where they are headed, so follow Michael Neill's advice. He says: "It starts by being clear about what kind of business you want for now, and knowing that it can change. I didn't start out wanting this big international business; I didn't have that sort of vision. I thought it would be fun to have work I liked to do. That's where I started. It's grown into what it is as a natural result of doing what I really wanted to do and enjoyed doing along the way. I'm such a believer in following your 'happy wanting'. When you are feeling good in yourself and you are feeling pretty clear in your thinking, you can just ask yourself questions like: 'What would be great? What would I love to have happen? What would I love to do? What would I love to create?' What I've found is that when you act on that kind of inspiration, wonderful things happen."

A great place to start to get the business skills is to find out what free or low-cost training is available to you. In addition, many other organisations offer paid-for training events, so take some time to look for opportunities available to you, and also find out what other people recommend before you invest your hard-earned cash.

Although this is covered in more detail in step 10, take some time to learn from the experts. If you are looking for a great marketer, find one and learn from them, go on training courses, listen to teleseminars or webcasts, engage with them on a one-to-one basis. Or find out who does something you want to do really well and discover more about that person and what makes them successful in what they do.

If you don't know much about business, marketing or public relations, expect to learn a lot about business in the early days. To put you on the right track, you will find a range of recommended resources in the back of this book.

Managing the financials and making a profit

'To attract money, you must focus on wealth. It is impossible to bring more money into your life when you are noticing you do not have enough, because that means you are thinking thoughts that you do not have enough.' – Rhonda Byrne

Many people forget that the purpose of being in business is to make a profit or create a financially viable business. But quite frankly, if you are not earning an income or making a profit, you won't be able to run your business for long. You won't have the mental capacity to stay focused on your clients as you will be worrying about how you are going to pay the next bills, or you may appear desperate when you are approached by a potential new client. Alternatively, if you start to create limiting beliefs about money, this will in turn limit your success.

There are various tools in this book to help you, but one of the things that came up in a couple of interviews, and also in my research around charging, is that people often run a coaching business to help people rather than to make money. I'm not saying that this is wrong, but you need to be able to charge what you are worth as well.

In my interview with Hannah McNamara on the subject, she said: "Money is important as you need to pay the bills, but what I have noticed in people who are starting out in coaching is that there's a lot of guilt attached to money. I think that is where people doubt their abilities to do the job and feel guilty for charging for something that they are not even sure they can do. I noticed that within myself as well. As my experience grew I started throwing out some of the bull***t that comes along with the early stages.

"I think as your experience grows in doing what you do, whether it's coaching, mentoring, training, or whatever, there's no guilt attached to charging for it – in fact you feel very grateful. I was asked by somebody to work on a Saturday and I said that will be double the price because I already had plans. It's actually quite enjoyable; it's a game, and the negotiations and things like that are fun. Just seeing how far you can push it. Then when they do agree, I think 'you could have asked for more.'"

In fact, to ease the pressure, many of the successful coaches I interviewed had a part-time job when they set up their business as it enabled them financial security, as well as the time to build their business as well. Suzy Greaves did some freelance journalism work. "It took ages – three years before I was actually making enough money that I didn't have to do journalism anymore," she said. "And even then it took me ages to find a business model and I'm about to change it again."

Hannah McNamara worked part time in a chair shop during her first year of business. For Hannah this was mainly due to the time lag in terms of obtaining clients. During that time she was aiming for corporate clients and she found that the time it takes to develop the relationship to the point that the client wants to buy could be eighteen months for corporate clients and for private clients, it could be six months.

Here is Hannah's advice during the early days: "You have to have a means of supporting yourself for the first year at least or be prepared to go and stack shelves. If your client is around during the day, do something in the evening to earn money or make sure you work your socks off for a couple of years beforehand and get enough money behind you so you can support yourself. There are outgoings in the first year. You've got to have your website; you've got to have your stationery. You've got to pay to go to networking events, you might pay to be listed on directory sites, you may want to invest in sending out mail shots and that all takes money. But I think some of this is coming from the way people perceive the training courses that they are going on. If you look carefully, all of these training courses will tell you that you are going to have to work for it, but people don't want to see that, they want to see that it is a quick thing, that they can quit their job on Friday and have a coaching business on Monday."

It is also important not to have so much money that you fail to take action in your business. As Blaire Palmer says: "People often provide too much of a cushion. They wait for redundancy, have a nice big redundancy payment and then there is no pressure to make the business work for the first two years as they have money. Then two years down the line they don't have the confidence to make it work because they haven't made it work already. When the money runs out they get a job. Then they will try and work part time but if the worse comes to the worse, they know they can increase their hours. Or they really reduce their overheads so they don't have to earn much money or their husband or wife supports them, so that now there is enough money, they don't have the motivation to make the business work." Blaire added: "For most people, you need some sort of rocket up you to make it happen. If you are not desperate and don't need it enough, you can't do the difficult things like go to the networking event, ask for the sale or charge enough."

Supercoach, Michael Neill, had this to say about money and profit: "I've always been a fan of being in profit from day one. There are other models in business, especially for big businesses, but for most of us starting out, money in needs to exceed money out. I know that shouldn't be a secret but apparently it is to a lot of people. The simple fact is that if you're not starting with money in the bank, growing through profits is one of the only sustainable models."

Michael went on to talk about setting fees: "Setting fees is something that a lot of people really struggle with, but it's completely unnecessary. In most cases, the market will bear whatever it is you tell it to. We're making up the market; there is no divine law that says we have to charge £200 a month. One of the great secrets that took me years to learn is that the more someone pays you to coach them, the better the results you will get. When I was first told that by one of my coaches, I thought it was offensive – I thought it was awful! But then I tried doubling my fees for all new clients. I was surprised that from the very first day my new clients were much more responsive, much more keen, and much more present than my previous clients had been – and that same pattern has held true until this day."

So I asked Michael how this applies to having his own coach. "At the moment, I pay my coach 150,000 USD a year, up front, in cash. Do you think I ever miss an appointment? Now please understand, he is also a brilliant coach; higher fees wouldn't work if he was just crap. But there's no question that I'm a better client for having paid so much. I just show up differently."

"The value of your coaching is not fixed in stone," he continued. "The value of your coaching is connected to how well you coach, but it is also influenced by how much you charge, the expectations you set, and the agreements you make with your clients. If you can even begin to see this, the difference it will make in your business will be huge."

Being a great coach

'Don't quack like a duck ... soar like an eagle.' – Ken Blanchard

As well as focusing on the pennies and becoming a business person, you need to be great at what you do. People are not going to employ you or refer you to someone else if you don't do the job you are employed to do.

I asked Michael Neill what his strategies are for running a successful coaching business. His first tip: "Be an amazing coach. It starts with your ability to make a difference. If you can't do that very well, work on your coaching, not on your business. One problem is that a lot of coaches don't get that coaching is a business, but there are also a number of coaches who don't seem to get that effective coaching is at the heart of the business. They put all their energy into marketing and getting a website, building their newsletter, raising their profile, but they are not very good coaches yet. First, learn how to change lives – then you can figure out the marketing."

His second tip: "It may seem obvious, but it's difficult to build a successful coaching business when your life sucks. Sort your own life out as you go, and this will free your energy to build your coaching business."

Taking these tips forward, take time to work on yourself as well as working on your clients, and learn how to be an amazing coach.

Suzy Greaves told me how she became a great coach: "I did everything I could within the first year to coach everyone with a pulse but it was really difficult because if you are coaching for free, people don't turn up, they're not motivated, and you constantly think you're failing, but the great thing about it is as you get so much practice, you get yourself out of the way." Later in our interview I asked Suzy how she can be the best coach she can be. "I create a space for that person to come into," she said, "and no matter what they tell me I'm not going to judge them. I am going to stand beside them and really hear them and really see them. That's why coaching is so brilliant, isn't it? The client is in a space where they are completely accepted for who they are, and taken on this journey to go and reach their potential."

As Steve Marriott summed up in our interview: "To be a coach, your track record is vital. I want people to be saying, 'Wow, I worked with Steve and this happened and it is *still* happening!' It is less about having great marketing materials and more about people saying, 'You really need to talk to this guy.' I haven't invested a penny in any type of physical marketing material since I started my business and I'm now in year five."

Steve Marriott also spoke about the three levels of coaching that Michael Neill talks about in his 'Supercoach' book. "Level 1 is that you simply apply a tool and get rid of a problem. Level 2 is that you give them a tool to apply in different areas of their life and level 3 is that you just change the way you think. A lot of people try for level 3 all of the time and it's just not appropriate – you've got to do what's right for your client. The times when you do a level 3 intervention you know that person will have a much better life."

Allison Marlowe sums up business success: "Personally, success to me is not about bringing in lots and lots of money, and I can see why people would define success in that particular way. Although it is about having enough to do the things I want to do without worry. Being successful is the satisfaction that I know I have done a good job in helping somebody overcome the problems, the issues that they have within their business, whether that's mindset, the confidence or whether that's the marketing side of that business, getting it up and getting it going. To me helping them achieve is a great success in my mind."

Duncan Brodie adds: "I think it is important to take the best bits out of everybody you connect with and craft that to be you. Throw your own bit in there and create your own mix. Ensure there is something that makes you stand out."

Overcoming objections

'Do not follow where the path may lead. Go instead where there is no path and leave a trail.' – Harold R. McAlindon

OK, I appreciate that some of you may be shouting at me right now. You may be saying I am a great coach, I have a great service but I am still struggling to make a profit and make my business work. One of the areas that many coaches struggle with is overcoming objections and converting potential clients, which contribute highly to creating a sustainable business.

If you follow the strategies in this book, they will help you to do this, so keep focusing on your success. Soon you will be even more successful like Steve Marriott who tells me, "I get bloody good outcomes, I never give up on people and I guess that's where the integrity comes in. I have to have a belief that that person will get there. I have to love my clients and care about them and their outcomes in order to help them get there. Otherwise I don't do it. I turn down as much as I take on. The relationship I build with people is important."

Gladeana McMahon: "You need to have the technical expertise to be able to really help people because your business will rise or fall on word of mouth. So you can always get people through the door through snazzy marketing techniques, but if you don't deliver, they won't come back and not only that, they will tell their friends not to bother. You also need to have a quality product, and never make promises you can't deliver on as that is vitally important too. In addition, you need to enjoy the business side of it as well."

Hannah McNamara: "No one wins any prizes for having ideas. There are a million other people who have had the same idea and are sitting back saying, 'That's my idea.' Well did you do anything about it? It's only going to happen when you make it happen and it's also about having a longer-term view. Keep a focus on what you want to do with this year, a few years down the track, and what you want to have in your five year plan."

Duncan Brodie: "Give things enough time to see if they are worthwhile. A lot of people do something once and if it doesn't work that's no good. Once you have set out your intention, keep doing it."

Let me leave you to think about this message from Michael Neill: "All you need to do to get a client is to have a conversation and that doesn't cost any money. Ironically, most people use 'marketing' to avoid having to have that conversation."

"You don't need fifty clients – you need one client," he says. "And when you've got that client, you don't need 49 clients – you need one client. And unless you are someone who is trying to create global domination instead of a successful coaching practice, it really is that simple."

NLP exercise – Changing your submodalities

Each of us represents our thoughts through our five senses, which make up our map of the world or personal reality. These are otherwise known as modalities or representational systems. Whilst using the modalities we each have a preference in how we learn and how we view the world.

You may prefer to use your visual sense (seeing aspects of life in pictures), others may be auditory (taking things in through hearing), and some may be kinaesthetic (how you feel about a situation). People also take things in through the olfactory (smell) or gustatory (taste) senses, but these are generally not the primary senses.

The modalities can be broken down further into finer distinctions called submodalities. Pictures may be still or moving, colours may be black and white or colour, bright or dull, clear or fuzzy. Sounds can be loud or soft; there may be differences in pitch and different tempos. Feelings can be hot or cold, be heavy or light and be in different parts of your body.

One thing that you can do is to change your submodalities by the way that you think about a situation. You can strengthen or weaken your personal representation of a situation by changing the way you sense the representation.

Let me use an example suited to becoming a business person.

If you have experienced a negative situation around a particular part of running your business, recall that situation now.

Picture yourself in this situation and change how you feel about the situation by changing your submodalities. For example, when you see the picture in your mind, change the colour; make it smaller. If it is clear, make the picture fuzzy; if it is a movie, turn it into a still picture. It will become less powerful if it is smaller, defocused and moved further away from you. If you are associated (seeing through your own eyes), disassociate yourself and watch yourself from a distance.

Consider the sounds that you heard in that situation. If what you hear is negative self-talk, turn down the volume of your voice. You could move it to a different place, turn it into a different, perhaps more motivating voice and change the language that it is using. Change the sounds that you hear.

If you feel in a particular way, change this too. If you feel heavy, become lighter. If you feel pressure, move the pressure, and you can change the texture, the size and any other parts of it.

What happens now?

_____

_____

_____

_____

Think of a pleasant experience and do the opposite to this. For example, bring the picture closer, turn black and white into colour and make it bigger. You can make similar changes to the auditory and kinaesthetic modalities too.

What happens now?

_____

_____

_____

_____

What this exercise does is to allow you to reframe situations using your different submodalities. You can change how you feel about a situation by changing your reaction to it.

Then you can use your pleasant experiences to intensify how you feel about these situations as well.

You use your submodalities to give meaning to your memories and although you cannot change the situation that has happened in the past, you can change your internal representation or response to that situation.

In addition, when you next want to succeed in a business situation, take some time to put yourself in that future situation in your mind. By changing your submodalities you will change the way you feel about the situation.

Now you have started to get a grasp of what it takes to be a business person and one of the most important parts of this is to develop your marketing skills. It is in these skills that all of the models excel, but used in different ways, and this is the topic for the next chapter.

Chapter 6 –
Step 4 Develop your marketing skills

'This may seem simple, but you need to give customers what they want, not what you think they want. And, if you do this, people will keep coming back.' – John Ilhan

Marketing skills are essential if you want to run a successful coaching business. In the early days of creating your business, you will be spending most of your time promoting your business. Whilst this is not purely a marketing book, I wanted to touch on some of the strategies that are used by coaches who run a successful business.

What is marketing?

'Marketing takes days to learn. Unfortunately it takes a lifetime to master.' – Philip Kotler

The Chartered Institute of Marketing (CIM) defines marketing as: 'The management process that identifies, anticipates and satisfies customer requirements profitably'. What this means is that you know what service or product you are providing to the customer, that this is what the customer wants and that you satisfy this need to enable you to satisfy the customer and make a profit for your business. In addition, your client first needs to know that you exist!

You may have heard of the marketing mix, which is made up of the 4 **P**s of marketing. Although there is much research which contradicts this early model, the basic concepts remain the same.

You need to have a tangible **product** or service. This will include your brand name, quality, type of service and how it is delivered. Whether this is a coaching service or tangible product, you need to specify what this is to enable you to market your business.

You will also need to know your **price**. This may be a pricing strategy dependent on different services or products, or a range of packages or programmes that you offer to your clients.

Place is also important as this is the action of getting the product or service to the customer. So you need to decide how you are going to provide the service to the customer, which may include one-to-one coaching, workshops, e-books, among other ways.

Promotion is the final of the 4 **P**s which includes aspects of marketing your business including your promotional strategy, advertising, and other forms of marketing.

Hannah McNamara runs HRM Coaching as well as the SME Academy with Dr Patrick White, a successful entrepreneur. As the author of *Niche Marketing for Coaches*, Hannah knows a thing or two about marketing.

About sales and marketing, Hannah says: "The part that is really overlooked by a lot of coaches is the sales part of it; and the business development. There is so much emphasis being placed on 'You've got to be on Twitter,' 'You've got to be on Facebook.' No – just get off your arse and go and meet people. Ring people up, ask for favours, ask if people will help you out. It's much easier to build a relationship by talking to somebody than by putting something out there expecting people to respond. And also things like Twitter; I'm on Twitter and I use it a lot but I use it for networking with other people who are well networked within my market – I don't ever use it to sell. I use it to follow others and to get updates. I've never expected someone to say, 'Ahh, fabulous update on Twitter, I'm going to hire you.' That's not going to happen."

"But I think within this market," Hannah continued, "people have got this idea that you can hide behind your computer, you can post some things in some forums and put things on Twitter and people are going to say, 'Ah yes, another coach, brilliant. I'm going to hire you.' The reality with social networking sites is that they are swamped, absolutely swamped, with coaches. What makes you successful in a coaching practice are your people-skills and getting out and talking to people and being able to explain what you do to them in a way that resonates with them and then they will respond. And I think that people are so afraid of rejection, it's just a bad fit. It's not the person that is rejecting you, it's either that the message is wrong or they are not in the right place for it yet or they need to work with somebody on this but they don't want to. It can take a couple of years for some people to come back to you and say, 'I met you at that thing a couple of years ago and something you said then I've remembered and I was going to come back to you'. You have to look at it as a long-term strategy; this isn't a get-rich-quick kind of business."

Provide what the client wants

'You can have the best product or service in the world, but if people don't buy – it's worthless. So in reality it doesn't matter how wonderful your new product or service is. The real question is – will they buy it?' – Noel Peebles

It is one thing to say, 'Hey I'm a great coach, and I know that I have a great workshop and I am going to market it to my potential clients,' but without knowing that your clients actually want this is a recipe for disaster. Many of the great coaches have learnt from doing this. So let me stress that it is essential that you find out what your clients want rather than what *you* think they want. Many coaches have wasted both time and money in designing and marketing events or services that nobody wants, or they don't sell the benefits of what they are offering.

So before you do anything, do your market research by following these steps:

Step 1: Define your customers. Who are they, what do they do, what problems do they face?
Step 2: Determine what you need to know about your customers. How can you reach these customers with your research?
Step 3: Choose a method of collating the data. You could do an offline or online survey (such as www.surveymonkey.com), contact focus groups, talk to your current clients, or pay for a market research company to do it for you, if this is within your budget.
Step 4: Find out what your successful competitors are doing and see what works for them.
Step 5: Analyse the data. Once you have all the data from your market research, analyse it and identify any trends. From this you should get a good overview of your customers and target market.
Step 6: Use the data and take action. Use the information to fine-tune your marketing plan and start your plan of action.

Clients don't buy coaching

'The aim of marketing is to know and understand the customer so well the product or service fits him and sells itself.' – Peter F. Drucker

You do need to know what the client wants and you do need to use effective marketing strategies. But importantly, you also need to know the features and benefits of what you offer to clients.

Clients don't buy coaching; they buy the result that they get from the intervention they use.

"They don't want to know about the techniques," Hannah McNamara says, "they just want you to do it to them. You don't ask a surgeon where they trained and everything like that, you just trust yourself and you trust that they know what they are doing and they will tell you what they need to do at a certain time and get on with it."

"It is not about trying to be different for difference sake," says Michael Neill. "It's not about trying to find your 'unique selling proposition'. What it is about is bringing your unique self, presence and insight to every coaching situation. If you are coaching from your soul, your being, your essence – no one else on the planet can coach like that. I can't – my coach can't. At that stage, people aren't coming to enquire about 'hiring a coach'; they're coming to find out about what it would take to hire you. This is why 'the market for coaches' is irrelevant. That market might be set in a certain place, but the market for *you* is wherever you say it is."

Many people find it hard to define the benefits of what they offer to clients, even if they are aware of the features of their service. To clarify, a feature is a characteristic of a product, and the benefits are what the customer has to gain by using the product or service, or simply how it will improve their situation. Have a go at the NLP exercise at the end of this chapter to find out more.

Marketing your business – so where do you start?

'Understand that you need to sell you and your ideas in order to advance your career, gain more respect, and increase your success, influence and income.' – Jay Abraham

As most of the model coaches I interviewed have a plan for their business, they have a plan for their marketing too. If they have a vision of where they want their business to be in one, two or five years' time, they will know how they can market themselves to achieve this.

There are various ways in which you can market your

business, which I will share with you in this section. As coaching is a service-based business, it is generally built on a foundation of relationship building, which is why some of these tactics will work and some will be less effective.

Advertising

Personally I have never found advertising to work for my business. To be successful, you need to be consistent in your advertising. Just placing a one-off advert in a paper or magazine is less likely to grab the attention of your potential clients, and is going to be costly too. However, regular advertising combined with other forms of marketing at the same time may work for you.

I asked Blaire Palmer what works for her. "Advertising is the coward's way," she said. "They will read about you, you get raised profile and credibility, but you don't get business. You get business from going out, meeting people face-to-face, and them taking a liking to you and thinking that you can help them to solve some problems."

Advertising also includes Google Adwords or other web-based pay-per-click advertising (PPC). This is an online way of putting your message in front of potential prospects when they search for the benefits that you offer, and you can limit the amount you pay for this service. Although this is a strategy used by many businesses, this method of marketing was not explicitly mentioned as a success strategy by any of the models I interviewed.

Networking

Networking is a great way to get recognised as a business person, and so much so that the next chapter is dedicated to helping you to do this. This can include both face-to-face meetings and social networking to help you to meet your potential clients, create joint ventures, get referrals and recommendations, and to build relationships with other like-minded people. Another way to get yourself recognised and remembered at networking events is to be the guest speaker, but more about that in the next chapter.

Cold calling

Cold calling is another way to market your business, but the thought often sends shudders down people's spines. So instead of cold calling, remember to follow up anyone who has been in contact with you, someone you have met at a networking event or a warm lead you have been given following a personal recommendation.

Website

The need to have a website before you market your business is a misconception, according to Michael Neill. As coaching is a service-based business, people buy people, so you just need to go out and market yourself. It helps to have a clear picture of your business, the service you offer and how you can help people, so having a website is a great place to start.

When I spoke to Steve Marriott he told me that he is in the process of building a website, and he has been running his successful business for more than four years.

However, many people will disagree and the advantages of having a website are that you have a presence on the internet which will allow you to build a dialogue with your targeted clients.

To build this dialogue, many of the most successful coaches have an electronic newsletter. Whether you want to send it out through your web provider or subscribe to Email Service Providers such as Infusionsoft, Constant Contact, Aweber, 1shoppingcart or something similar, this is a great way to get a following and start to build your business. People who sign up to a newsletter are usually attracted by a free gift, perhaps an e-course or e-book then agree to sign up to your newsletter. Although you might think, 'OK now I have a list, let's create business,' yes you can indeed market your products to your list, but you also need to provide value and interesting content.

I spoke to Suzy Greaves about how she creates her subscriber list. "It's about creating a tribe," said Suzy, "a tribe that you can head up and have a dialogue with and give them value. You are part of a community; you've got to give as well – you can't just take. So I would say building a database and having a vibrant and dynamic conversation with that database is key. I think newsletters do work, but it creates a lot of energy to write a newsletter and I find it better to do something quick and often twice a week sending something like: 'Have you seen this?' or 'Have you done that?' or creating a programme they can work through."

Also remember that a list does have to be permission based and that those who sign up to your newsletter need to agree to opt in. You can build your list of contacts through a range of ways, through speaking, networking and building relationships through workshops, training and your one-to-one work.

As far as online marketing is concerned, another way to reach your audience is through writing articles. Online article sites such as www.ezinearticles.com are great sites for you to showcase your expertise. Duncan Brodie has over three hundred articles that he has published through this medium. But the trick is to be able to recycle or reuse what you have written. If you have written an article, it can be included in your newsletter, blog, ezine article, in the local or national press, as part of developing workshops or training sessions to name but a few areas to consider.

Media coverage

Media coverage can take many forms, from a press release about a new product or service you have released, to an article or even a book you have had published. The advantage of media coverage, as long as it is favourable and informative, is that your message will reach a wide audience. Both Suzy Greaves and Blaire Palmer come from a media background, in fact Blaire actually became a coach after running a piece about coaching during her media career. She carried out an interview with Ginny Bailey and held a live debate with Laura Berman-Fortgang.

I asked Suzy whether her background has helped her. "Yes it has massively," she said. "I was thinking that the other day. My ability to write well has served me really well. But writing might not be your best skill; you might have other skills like speaking instead."

Suzy's advice for getting published is as follows: "When selling yourself in the press, it's never about you. No one's interested in you, no one's interested in your coaching practice; it's about the story, the case history or whatever."

Most of the coaches I interviewed have written in some form or another, whether these are articles for the press or for magazines, and some are published authors. In addition, Dawn Breslin and Gladeana McMahon appear regularly on the television. However you wish to raise your profile, getting in touch with local and national papers and magazines that are bought by your target market are great places to start.

Direct mail

Direct mail is another strategy you can try, and it is possible to buy lists of contacts to enable you to do this easily. However, like cold calling, unless you already have a named contact to follow up, a letter may well end up in the bin. The secret is to build relationships, so if you do send a letter, follow it up with a phone call and secure a meeting with the person you wish to meet.

Promotional material

One of the mistakes that many coaches and trainers make is

having very expensive flyers or brochures printed during the early days because you may find that your message changes as your business develops. That's not to say that having a professional appearance isn't important, but make sure that you have clearly defined what you do before you spend a lot of money on literature that you don't really need.

Building relationships with people

In essence, all the business and marketing techniques are there to help you to build relationships with people, whether they become clients, associates or friends. "I always follow up and keep relationships going on an individual basis," says Marian Way. "Although I haven't yet cracked how to attract a lot of people, I am good at keeping in touch with people, which is just as important as they start recommending me to others. There is also something about the quality of what you do with the clients you do have. The workbooks I produce, the flipcharts, and the way I work with people all help to keep people coming back for more."

What else you need to know

Another thing you will need to consider is where you are currently in your business, whether you are in the early stages or reaching maturity, as different marketing strategies will work during different stages. In addition, you may have a tendency towards a preferred style of contacting people, whether you prefer talking to people face-to-face or via the telephone.

In C.J. Hayden's book, *Get Clients Now!*, C.J. recommends developing your own personal 28 day sales and marketing programme, where you can pick and choose ingredients for your marketing plan. So this means that if you are in the early days of running your business, you may be filling your pipeline of potential contacts, clients and connections. Later on in your business you may well be spending your time following up contacts, making presentations or closing the sale.

What I love about C.J.'s book is that she allows you to pick and choose how you carry out your marketing based upon your strengths and your skills. You can speak, cold call, do internet marketing, network and many other forms of marketing to make a plan for your business success.

NLP exercise – Stepping Up

This exercise is a variation of the NLP exercise, Stepping Up. Two versions are outlined below and you can choose which one you prefer to use to determine the features and benefits of your service or product. Ideally work with a partner so they can help you to record your responses.

Make a list of the features (the facts) of your service or product, which are the aspects of the product or service that you sell. Once you have this list of features you can start to discover the benefit of each feature by making the statement ... 'which means' ... when talking about each feature of your service. The benefits are about the results the client will get from this feature and how it improves their lives. For example, you are not selling coaching; you are selling the experience, results and solutions that your client gets from working with you.

Alternatively you can follow the NLP exercise Stepping Up. To enable you to come up with the most important benefit you can offer a client, after each phrase or word you come up with, ask yourself (ideally do this with a partner): *What will that give them?* You will soon have a long list of benefits that will support the way you market your services to a potential client.

Let me challenge you now to do one of these exercises. Think about a product or service that you are currently offering to your clients. By using one of the exercises above, list 10 benefits to the client of using that product or service.

1.

2.

3.

4.

5.

6.

7.

8.

9.

10.

What have you learnt?

_____

_____

_____

What are you going to do differently?

_____

_____

_____

I hope that this exercise helped you to start to hone down the benefits of what you offer your clients, as they do buy the benefits to them rather than coaching or the features of what you offer. They don't necessarily need to know how you do it, but are more interested with the results you give them. So now we move on to another important area to help you to transform your business, and that is to develop your networks.

Chapter 7 –
Step 5 Develop your networks

'80% of success is just turning up.' – Woody Allen

An essential part of running a business, networking is the act of meeting people in a business or social context. It gives you the opportunity to share ideas and information and meet potential business partners or clients. Although it can be quite daunting for someone who has never done any networking before, it is an important business skill for coaches and it can bring about many benefits for your business as well, such as referrals, connections and joint ventures, especially during the early days in business.

Why must you network?

'The way of the world is meeting people through other people.' – Robert Kerrigan

There are various reasons why networking is essential for your business. It has many advantages:

- You can meet people who may be of help to you or other people you know. As a coach, it can be isolating when you work alone, so building your network of potential colleagues, friends or associates is hugely rewarding. Personally, I enjoy connecting other people and my networks enable me to do this effectively.

- You can collect the contact information of people you meet, which will enable you to contact them for potential new opportunities or pass their information on to other people. Having a large network of contacts will also enable you to grow your business quicker, as people who know, like and trust you are more likely to refer or recommend you to others.

- To keep in touch with people in your network, whether these are local business owners or other coaches, trainers, or consultants. This may lead to joint ventures and sales.

- To find out more about your competitors, as well as collecting relevant information relating to your industry or profession.

- Often there will be the opportunity to learn, as many networking events will have a speaker or purpose for the event, and the chance to meet new people.

- As statistics show that everyone knows an average of two hundred and fifty people, if you need to connect with a particular person, you are bound to know someone who can put you in touch. Also if you believe in the six degrees of separation (also referred to as the 'human web') everyone is at most six steps away from any other person on Earth. So if you want to connect with someone, just ask your network.

Networking can give you a range of opportunities, including meeting people in a formal networking meeting, using social media or in informal situations by talking to people about what you do.

Meeting people in the flesh

'It isn't just what you know, and it isn't just who you know.

It's actually who you know, who knows you, and what you do for a living.' – Bob Burg

As I have indicated earlier in this chapter, all of my models agree that you need to meet people to develop your business. Find out what networks you have in your area, and try them out. You can do this via the internet, social media or just by asking other people you know in business. Most areas have a range of networks including breakfast meetings such as Business Networking International (BNI) or something similar, local Chamber of Commerce, business exhibitions and trade fares, lunchtime meetings, coffee meetings and evening networks.

Some of these networks may be more formal than others. You may wish to experiment in the beginning to find out what networking groups work for you. In my early days I quickly found out which networking groups were comfortable and ones which I did not enjoy attending.

When Clean Language coach, Marian Way set up Apricot Island she joined BNI for a period. "That helped a lot," said Marian, "not in terms of getting hundreds of clients, but because it made me feel like I was a business. Every Monday morning I had to stand and say, 'My name's Marian Way and my business is called Apricot Island.' It made me believe that I was a business. I did get some clients and I met people I am still working with now."

Due to other commitments Marian did not continue attending the BNI meetings, but later found networking groups that enabled her to connect with her target market – predominantly coaches. "It didn't occur to me at the time to go to these coaching groups," she said. "And part of that was because at BNI there is this whole mentality about not wanting more than one particular 'specialist' in the group. Only one coach, only one trainer etc. You've got to keep it all to yourself. There was not an abundance mentality – there was a 'shut out your competitor' mentality. So I had shut out coaches, and I did not cotton on that they were my market for training. When I started to meet more coaches, of course I discovered that they are perfectly lovely people, many of whom want to learn Clean Language."

Hannah McNamara's advice is: "You have to do it if you want to get out there and if for the first few years you've got to get out and network, well, you go to breakfast, lunches, evening things – you just do it."

However, be selective about the type of networking events you go to. Here is some advice from Blaire Palmer: "If you spend time with other people, make sure it is not necessarily with other coaches. That helps with the mindset as you start to see yourself as a business person and not just a coach."

How to 'do' networking

'The successful networkers I know, the ones receiving tons of referrals and feeling truly happy about themselves, continually put the other person's needs ahead of their own.' – Bob Burg

As a coach, you should be good at meeting people at networking events because two of the greatest skills required are the abilities to listen well and ask questions. When you meet someone new, start with the objective of finding out more about them by asking open questions and this will allow you to build good relationships. If you can confidently introduce yourself, introduce other people, remember people's names, ask powerful questions and actively listen to the responses, you have made a good start.

If you have never attended any networking events before, you may well be nervous or not sure of the protocol required. As every networking event is different, you will have to adapt your style, but here are some tips for you:

Know who is attending

One of the tips advised by the top networkers is to get the

delegate list in advance and scan for people you know and those you would like to meet. You can then do some research about them as well as being informed in advance.

Choose the right networking group and always go with an intention

Networking can take a lot of time and money and you will do a lot of it especially during the early days of running your business. So it is important to have an intention for spending your time and money, and specifically which networking groups are best for you.

Leadership Coach, Duncan Brodie: "With your networking, it is important to be targeted. Go to networking groups where people in your target market are. When I do anything locally, that is the intention I go with. I tend to do a lot of accountancy bodies meetings and I will do the Chamber of Commerce occasionally. I go to the Chamber of Commerce with an intention, perhaps to go to find potential referral partners or joint venture partners; I'm not going to find any clients, so I focus on getting to know people.

"It's about finding out where your folks hang out and take it from there. There's not much point in doing everything. A lot of people say BNI and that sort of stuff is good, and it is for some professions. It's got some merits but what you've got to really think about is not the cost element, but the time commitment. Can you afford to give out a hundred to a hundred and fifty odd hours a year? That's seven days a year, give or take."

Steve Marriott told me that a great way to meet new clients is to go to networking meetings and quality learning events. "At these events," he says, "people are open-minded and curious. They explore a lot more, so that initial meeting is a better quality. I get massive referrals and a lot of return work as well, particularly when I've been working with large organisations and they recommend me. I create a reputation and partnership with an organisation so why would they go anywhere else?"

One thing I urge you to think about when attending a networking event is that it is not the place to force your business card on to someone else, but it is better to request the card of the other person which allows you to follow up with them after the meeting. Then remember to follow up!

Be consistent

One aspect that a couple of the interviewees mentioned to me is to be consistent. Also, once you have found the network for you – persevere. Instead of attending loads of networking events once, find a few that you enjoy going to and consistently build relationships with the people there. Also once you have gained a great relationship with the host and want to meet a particular person, let them know and I'm sure they will help you out.

Develop your perfect pitch

Networking is about building relationships, sharing knowledge and gaining information. One of the things you will need when you attend a networking event is an elevator pitch. An elevator pitch is so named as it is the short introduction you can carry out in the time span of a ride in a lift or elevator, which is around thirty seconds. Your pitch is something you will use when you meet someone for the first time, when you are introducing yourself formally to a group or when you are giving a speech or presentation.

Developing the perfect pitch is something that you need to take time over. The purpose is to promote you and your business and generally answers questions such as what your business, service or product is, and the benefits of this business, service or product. It needs to be simple, concise, clear and well practised. In addition, it is not a sales pitch, but aims to get the person listening to ask the question: 'How do you do that then?'

Marketing Expert, Rachel O'Reilly from Morph PR has given me permission to publish her top 10 tips to help you to develop your perfect pitch.

The Perfect Pitch

1. Short and memorable
2. Get people interested in you
3. No job titles or jargon
4. Get them to ask you about it – make them want to ask, 'How?' as soon as you finish
5. Avoid things which they might have preconceived ideas about – coach, consultant, etc
6. Paint a memorable picture which includes them
7. Find common ground, or something they can relate to
8. Sell them the benefits rather than the features of your product or service
9. Believe it or it just won't work
10. Head up, shoulders back, breathe and smile!

I would recommend two sentences maximum.

© Morph PR 2010 (www.morphpr.com)

Developing valuable contacts

The most important thing about networking is that you are attending to meet with like-minded people and not going just to sell to them. You will often develop personal relationships within your networks of people and opportunities for meeting up for coffee or lunch and helping each other out.

"I tend to do a bit of social networking," said Duncan Brodie, "but what I have started doing quite a lot recently is having virtual coffees. You have a cup of coffee, they have a cup of coffee and you connect on Skype. It is virtual as you are not meeting them face-to-face but it is a good way of connecting and sharing."

Speaking at networking groups

Another way to network is to speak at networking events. This is a strategy used by many of the models. Although you will often not be paid significantly, if at all, speaking at networking events is a great platform for building your business. As well as allowing the audience to pick up useful information during a networking event, it positions you as an expert in your subject.

Duncan Brodie regularly speaks at accountancy networking events and Hannah McNamara regularly talks at events such as those run by Business Link, Chamber of Commerce, Women's groups, and other big events.

Allison Marlowe runs her own networking event, called Hampshire Winning Women and the group meet once a month in Fareham, Hampshire, and she is regularly on the lookout for speakers for her networking events. Allison's advice is to decide what you want to achieve from speaking at networking events and what you want to get from the participants. She says that you should always find a method to collect contact details to allow you to follow up later as well as filtering out warm and cold leads. You could do this by offering a prize to people who put their business cards in a box from which a winner is selected, by asking participants to complete an evaluation form or by selling a product at the back of the room.

Admittedly, if you are nervous at attending networking events, you may be even more petrified at speaking at networking events in front of a group, but like everything, it takes practice and stepping outside of your comfort zone to be more successful.

Social networking

Another form of networking is social networking. This covers a plethora of platforms that you may or may not have heard of, including:

- Facebook
- Twitter
- LinkedIn
- Plaxo
- You Tube
- Ecademy
- Myspace
- Flickr
- Bebo
- Ning groups, such as Giant Potential

Please note that this list is not exhaustive and highlights just some of the most popular sites. All of the coaches I interviewed use social networking as part of their business model although some more prominently than others.

Duncan Brodie's advice: "Take a few things and do them well. I don't think that you can do more than three really well. I do Facebook, Twitter and LinkedIn. A lot of people have signed up for all of these things for the back links which is completely the wrong reason to do it."

In addition, you may also have heard of blogging. A hugely popular tool, this also factors under social networking. The advantages of blogging are that search engines such as Google love updated content and this will push your website higher up the rankings. So a regularly updated blog through Blogger, Wordpress or one of the other blogging platforms will help to develop your business and again position you as an expert in your field, provided that good quality information is posted.

In Chapter 6, I mentioned that Hannah McNamara stated that although social networking is good to build relationships online, it doesn't beat face-to-face networking.

What it does do, however, is allow you to keep in touch with business acquaintances, as it is a hugely popular communication tool. The downside is that it is easy to waste many hours on these sites when it would be better use of your time meeting people or undertaking other activities to build your business.

When using social media, it is important to remember:

- Your postings are highly visible so it is important to consider what you post before you press submit.
- You need to make sure that you have appropriate privacy settings to protect yourself against identify theft as well as from sharing too much information.
- Some social media sites allow you to set up a business page as well as a personal page, so you can separate the two identities.
- You can spread yourself too thinly, so take Duncan Brodie's advice and spend your time on two or three sites you can do well.
- Many social networking sites allow you to put a posting on multiple sites at the same time, which saves you time and energy.

Ultimately, networking is about building relationships, sharing great information, connecting people and also enjoying yourself of course!

NLP Exercise - Anchoring confidence

One of the aspects that put people off face-to-face networking is having the confidence to actually do it. There is a great NLP technique called anchoring, which you can use every time you go to a networking meeting, so now there is no excuse!

Every experience that we take in includes some or all of our five senses: visual (see), auditory (hear), kinaesthetic (feel), olfactory (smell) and gustatory (taste). Anchoring refers to a trigger that can be applied to produce a positive state and change your behaviour in a situation. Anchors occur naturally in everyday life. For example, if you hear a song on the radio, it may remind you of a particular experience where you heard that song, and will trigger the associations of that experience.

The great thing about this technique is that you can anchor a resourceful state that you can trigger whenever you want it. Within this example, the state being anchored is confidence, but this exercise can be used to create other resourceful states, such as relaxation or calmness.

Here is the first exercise to help you to recreate the feeling of confidence when you walk into the next networking meeting or any other situation when you wish to be in this state. This is a traditional anchor, and there is a second exercise, called the circle of excellence which is another form of anchoring, detailed below. Go through each of the steps below to anchor your confident feeling.

1. Remember a time when you felt really confident. NB If you find this difficult, think of a time in the future when you wish to be in this state and how you would feel.
2. Associate yourself into this experience by seeing the situation through your own eyes. Hear what you heard, feel what you felt and see what you saw.
3. Intensify this state. Make the colours bigger, brighter and bolder, the feelings more intense and the sounds even louder.
4. At the peak of the experience, anchor the feeling, by touching a part of your body that you can easily

access discreetly when you need to resource this experience again (e.g. touching the thumb and forefinger on your left hand).

5. Once you have anchored the state, take yourself out of the resourceful state and briefly change your state by undertaking a different activity.
6. Repeat steps 1-5 three times. Test the anchor by touching your body at the part where you anchored it and the confident state will return.
7. You can make the anchor stronger by practising this exercise again daily over a few weeks. You can also stack the anchor by remembering other vivid confident experiences and following the process above using the different experiences and the same anchor point.
8. Then when you are about to attend your next networking event, visualise how confident you will be, and what you see, feel and hear.

Just one more point. To be effective, here are 4 rules of effective anchoring:

1. It should be timed just as the state is reaching its peak.
2. It should be linked to a state that is cleanly and completely experienced.
3. The anchor should be unique and easily replicated.
4. The person needs to be associated and the experience intense.

In addition you can create different anchor points for different resourceful states that you would like to create.

Circle of excellence

The circle of excellence is another NLP technique that you can use to create a confidence anchor. The difference between the first exercise and this one is that this is a spatial anchor, which means that it requires you to move to physically to create the anchor.

1. Like the first anchoring exercise, think of a situation where you would like to be more confident (or have another resourceful state). Make an imaginary circle on the floor which is large enough for you to step into.
2. Think of all the resources that you would like to have to enable you to behave or think in the way you would like to behave or think in that situation.
3. Taking each resource in turn, remember an occasion when you had that resource and then put yourself into that memory. Associate yourself into this experience by seeing the situation through your own eyes. Hear what you heard, feel what you felt and see what you saw.
4. Take this state into your circle of excellence and stay there for a few moments in the fully resourceful state. Then step out of the circle.
5. Change your physiology and then test the anchor by stepping into your circle of excellence. Notice what happens when you do this. Then step out.
6. Now step into the circle and notice how you will be different in the future in the way you think about the situation you want to change, e.g. your feeling of confidence when walking into a networking event.
7. Remember to pick up your circle and take it with you and use it when you need it.

So now you have a couple of great resources you can use to be confident whenever you need to walk into a room full of strangers and some great ideas to connect with your potential clients. So let's move on to your business itself.

Chapter 8 –
Step 6 Be an expert in your field

'The talent of success is nothing more than doing what you can do, well.' – Henry W. Longfellow

There are many schools of thought about whether you need to be an expert in the field in which you coach. When I did my coaching training, the message I received is that trained coaches can coach anyone. I agree up to a point that sometimes it helps if you don't know much about a subject as you can remain impartial and not allow your own experiences to get in the way of the coaching session. However, I also believe that clients usually seek out a particular type of coach to get a solution around an area of concern and will seek an expert in that field.

If you are an expert in your area, this allows you to market yourself more effectively as you can position yourself as that expert. In addition you can specify the types of results that you are able to achieve with the client.

To niche or not to niche

'What is it that you like doing? If you don't like it, get out of it, because you'll be lousy at it. You don't have to stay with a job for the rest of your life, because if you don't like it you'll never be successful in it.' – Lee Lacocca

This is a topic I raised with many of my models, and to be honest, I have received conflicting answers. We are advised at an early stage in our business development to identify with a clear niche which is specific.

In Hannah McNamara's book, *Niche Marketing for Coaches*, Hannah talks about two different ways to approach choosing a niche. The first is niche coaching and the second is niche marketing. She defines niche coaching as 'coaching in an area such as parenting, career, fitness, wealth, small business coaching' among many other areas. Quoting the Chartered Institute of Marketing, she defines niche marketing as 'the marketing of a product to a small and well defined segment of the market place'. So this process would be to 'aim your marketing to a specific group of people who have something in common', which could be doctors, accountants, human resources professionals, dentists, or a group of people such as working mothers or managers seeking promotion.

"Think in terms of niche marketing first," says Hannah, "and then think about niche coaching. It is much easier to start with the kind of people that you want to coach and then consider the challenges that they may be facing. Of course, you could think about it the other way round if you already have a type of coaching that you're passionate about and good at. Then you can think about what types of people are most likely to want coaching on that topic or issue."

Some of the interviewees did not have a clear niche at the start. I asked Leadership Coach Duncan Brodie about his niche: "I have one now," he said. "I didn't when I started. When I started out, if they had a pulse, I coached them. One of the things I realised is that only 5% of the population will consider working with a coach. That's quite an Insight. That was a real wake-up call and I thought to myself, actually 12 months before I started out, I didn't know about coaching. The challenge for coaches is to start to see coaching as a tool and the results as the thing that the client actually wants."

On the subject of niching, Marian Way said: "If I were to take on a coach to help me with my marketing, I would jolly well expect them to know about marketing. Although I would be perfectly happy to go to a Clean Language coach about marketing too, as I am aware that I know stuff that I don't think I know."

"One of the weird things about setting up as a coach on my own is to put a tag on what I did," said Steve Marrriott. "I'd never been able to make that differential, and call myself a Success Coach. I have worked with people with relationship problems, parenting issues, professionals requiring career advice, and it depends on the person and what their needs are at the time. I work with people to help them to create more choices. Rather than feeling a victim of circumstance I help them work through it. The more tangible their success is, the easier it becomes.

"It is important for coaches to work with people they genuinely care about and doing work that they feel adds value. If you don't, you won't be performing at your best. I believe my business is beneficial to those people I work with. I provide the absolute best value and that's not about cutting costs, it's about the fact that you won't get a better outcome with anyone else. It is important for me to work in partnership with them. It is important that I care about them and that everyone is explicitly clear with the expectations and the outcomes.

"Niching is the biggest mistake that coaches make unless you genuinely have one you love," continued Steve. "People have been told they should niche, that they should go 'narrow but deep'. You are the expert on you. You are the only one who knows if the shoe fits. For most coaches, especially early in their careers, niching is a mistake. The only way you can work it out is by coaching everyone that appeals. It's a process of discovery."

Michael Neill: "When I started, I coached anybody. People asked: 'What's your niche?' and I said: 'People who can pay me.' And then I became a little more comfortable with what I was doing and my niche became 'people who can pay me that I like'. And then it became 'people who really want to work with me as opposed to just working with a coach'. And it continues to evolve. I know no greater joy than facilitating the happiness and wellbeing of another human being and giving people the support to create what they want most in their lives."

Blaire Palmer: "I think you can coach everybody, but whether you want to is another thing. I find certain types of coaching very boring; I don't enjoy career coaching, so I refer those people on. I think the skills around asking questions and listening are completely transferable and in fact the less you know about the subject, the better coach you can be sometimes as you don't make all the same assumptions about the subject as the person you are coaching. So always say you are not an expert in anything except being able to elicit the expertise from the other person. Having said that, I increasingly see myself as an expert in behaviour and organisational change, not that I can tell people what to do, but I can give some ideas about how they can go about finding out what to do. So I'm less pure as a coach these days where I am more confident as I've seen something similar many times before. But I am still very detached from my advice."

The advantages of having a niche are that you can clearly define the pain of your target audience and know how you can help them to turn the pain into pleasure. Also it allows you a clear way of marketing what you do and who you can help. I know that during the early stages, many new coaches don't wish to have a niche as they don't want to restrict the clients that they can help. However, if you know how you can help people it makes the whole area of business development, marketing and networking so much easier to undertake.

On the flip side, your niche may well change as you develop your business as you will find that you like working with a particular type of person or in a specific niche area. Allison Marlowe is a particular example of this. When she started her business she was a parent coach but quickly found that many people were coming to her with issues around starting and running small businesses. After three years of running her business, she rebranded as a Women's Business Coach.

Adding your own ingredients to the mix

'An expert is someone who has succeeded in making decisions and judgements simpler through knowing what to pay attention to and what to ignore.' – Edward De Bono

When you are deciding whether to niche, or indeed in what area to niche, it is important to add your own ingredients to the mix. In what areas are you an expert? What is your background? There is not much point in specialising in an area that you will not enjoy, so what inspires you or excites you?

Suzy Greaves told me that it is important to get a niche that you are passionate about. "Write a book," she says. "Become an expert and then write articles and become known in the press as the 'go-to person' for that."

You may also want to consider:

Your experience and expertise

If you choose to niche in a particular area, start by drawing on your experience and expertise. If this is an area that inspires you it might be worth concentrating on this first. The advantages are that you may well have contacts in this area. You are likely to know the types of clients and their pain and how you can help them to achieve what they want.

Your strengths and skills

Also consider your strengths and your skills and how these can be used to create a successful business. You can start by completing a personal SWOT analysis where you can start to understand your strengths, weaknesses, opportunities and threats.

Whether you have a hungry crowd

I am sure you want to create a business that is viable, sustainable, and ideally profitable. With this in mind, you need to ensure you have a hungry crowd of people who want your services. Start by conducting market research with people in the area you have chosen, and find out more about your potential clients' needs.

Women's Business Coach, Allison Marlowe spoke to me about the well known BBC programme Dragon's Den. "There are hundreds of people out there who come up with a fantastic, innovative idea," she said, "and they are never going to get anywhere as there is no demand for it. They often have that self-belief, but what is probably lacking is the marketing and business side of it."

How you will market yourself

As I mentioned earlier in this book, people don't buy coaching – they buy the results that coaching brings. What are the results you can deliver to your clients?

Being unique

You can learn many things from the experts, but you also need to be unique as a coach in terms of your personality that you bring to your clients. People buy people, and what might work for one potential client might not work for another. It will often take a while to develop your personality and Hannah McNamara reflects on a personal story: "People need to be comfortable about bringing in their personality, especially in the early days when people are still learning their technique as they feel very self-conscious about that. I have a long-standing client and he told me that in the early days I was very formulaic. He knew that five minutes before the end I was going to ask him this and when I said this sort of thing, he would say that. But because we got to know each other, although he still says he knows very little about me, and what I do outside of sessions because we don't talk about it, he knows my personality. So I think that's what it's all about."

What needs to be in your toolkit?

'We know what we are, but know not what we may be.' – William Shakespeare

As you are reading this book, I assume that you are a coach, trainer or consultant who is undertaking or has completed a coaching qualification, or perhaps you run another service-based business. If this is the case, you may also wish to consider what other tools you need in your toolkit. Although I have dedicated a whole chapter to your ongoing learning and development, there are other tools you might need to consider now.

Once you have decided what types of clients you want to work with and how you can help them, you might need to do more learning to enable you to meet these needs; for example, this may include presentation or facilitation skills. Or perhaps you want to be able to signpost people to other resources that could help them, such as books or websites, which will require more research and time.

In addition, you may find that you need to learn more about the different technologies and platforms for coaching, such as Skype, social media, video, audio, teleseminars or online coaching platforms such as JigsawBox and membership sites.

Or you may wish to undertake more personal learning and development, such as NLP, to grow your toolkit and the solutions you can offer your clients. But more about that in Chapter 10.

Michael Neill spoke about his toolkit: "My first professional coach training was fantastic at getting me started, but I then went on to train in a number of other programmes and that training still goes on today. Why so much training? Because if you have eight ways of being stuck and I have nine ways of getting you unstuck, I win – and so do you!"

Resources and support

'Be the change you want to see in the world.' – Gandhi

During the early stages of running your coaching business, it is unlikely that you can afford a huge amount of resources or support. But as you develop your business, you may find that it makes sense to get help with various aspects of work, especially areas in which you do not personally excel.

The most valuable investment that I have made in my own business is to have a business coach and mentor. Although this can seem an unnecessary expense during the early stages, I have found it essential for my own success, and most of my models agree.

"I think I invest more on my mentoring than I do on my marketing," says Allison Marlowe. "That's how highly I value that and learn from other successful people. I wouldn't ever like to say that I copy them but I do model them. I think it is important to be authentic but there are certain strategies, methods that do work and if you can learn those from somebody else who is achieving great results, it saves you an awful lot of time, energy, and money."

If you cannot afford a business coach or mentor right now, there are plenty of people who you can follow. Duncan Brodie recommends Robert Middleton, Bernadette Doyle and Steve Mittern.

Supervision is another area in which many coaches seek support. Parent Coach, Suparna Dhar believes that supervision is important. As she coaches parents in disadvantaged communities, having a supervisor is an essential part of her business.

Marian Way goes to events run by her Clean Language mentors, Penny Tompkins and James Lawley. "It is having a place where you can be yourself," Marian said, "where you are not trying to be that business person, where you can let any of that go and just be who you are fully and with other people. We do Clean Language and modelling activities and it's fabulous. I'm not being Marian from Apricot Island when I go there. I'm just me. And it's great and I think people need that. We all hide parts of our personality in different contexts. It is important for coaches to have somewhere where you can let your guard down and be yourself, as it can feel like you are supposed to be super human and we're not."

For Gladeana McMahon, she values having lots of good people around her. "I believe in having experts and having people I trust around me," she says, "and when I have people like that, I trust them to get on with it. At the moment, my Executive Assistant and my cleaner are the most important people in my life, because they hold the infrastructure together. We might be the clever ones on paper but they're the ones that make it easier to do the work I do; they're the glue and people forget things like that."

On the subject of the other experts Gladeana works with, she said: "I've got a team of cognitive behavioural therapists and coaches so they run the whole of the referral side for people who choose not to see me because there is a price differential. Always have a good accountant – that is absolutely crucial, and make sure that you take their advice as well. I have a television agent and I have people I can consult in the book world. So that's what I mean about having experts around. I have a computer chap who comes in once a month to maintain my computer system as I'm hugely dependent on it. It's having the right people in place and knowing where to get the people if you haven't already got someone."

To summarise, some important resources you may have in your business are:

- A business coach or mentor and perhaps a personal coach as well
- A supervisor
- An executive assistant or Virtual Assistant (who works with other businesses as well, where you can usually pay by the job or the hour)
- An accountant or book-keeper
- A reliable IT person
- A marketing or business expert
- Other business people or joint venture partners who may be complementary to your business.

Remember as much as you are a great coach, other people may be better at doing some of the other things in your business. If you can outsource the work to others, this frees up your time to support your clients and develop your business.

But also take advice from Marketing Expert, Hannah McNamara. "We've all got things that we don't enjoy doing, but we've got to do," she says. "As you get more established and have the revenue to support it, it's easier to outsource those sorts of things, and then just play to your strengths. Of course you can get someone else to do things, but that's not realistic for someone who doesn't have the money to pay their own bills. You're not going to take on a member of staff if you can't pay yourself."

NLP Exercise – perceptual positions

We naturally take different positions at different times in our lives. This is a great exercise that you can use if you want to see things from another point of view. This will allow you to step into another person's shoes and see the world from their perspective. It enables you to open up greater levels of understanding. You can use it for when there is a block in understanding between two people or if you feel stuck about a situation.

Work with a partner, who will stand and observe the exercise and give you feedback after you have completed each step.

Set out three chairs or allocate three positions on the floor:

- The first position is your perspective on the situation.
- The second position is another person's perspective.
- The third position is a third perspective on the situation or observer.

Decide what situation or issue you would like to work with and change for the better. Go to the first position and tell your partner what you feel about the situation. This will include your opinions, your views about events, your related values and beliefs, and how you feel about a situation including any difficulties.

Then move to the second position and become the other person and put yourself in their position. For example, how is that person thinking about the same situation? It would be useful if you could adopt the physiology of this person to give his or her point of view, including reacting to some of the things said from the first position about the situation.

Then move to the third position and comment as an observer, looking at both persons in the first and second positions. You may wish to give advice to both parties.

Take time to visit the first and second positions again to see how the situation changes as you see it from different perspectives. Then end in the first position and notice what you have learnt about yourself and the situation. Consider what new choices you have available to you now. Then swap over so both people complete the exercise.

The aim of the exercise is to see a situation from different perspectives, to notice how your view of it may change, and to perhaps come up with some ideas for how to modify your behaviour. Although it is not possible to offer advice to the second position person, changing your perception will inevitably alter the communication in the real world.

By now you should have developed a greater sense of purpose for your coaching business. You have a greater understanding of the business skills required and the sense of what you need to do, so the next step is to create a plan for your business.

Chapter 9 –
Step 7 Start with the end in mind

'It pays to plan ahead. It wasn't raining when Noah built the ark.' – Author unknown

When I first qualified as a coach in 2006, I didn't have a vision for my business. I didn't know which way I was headed, which made it pretty hard to get there.

So the advice in this chapter is to start with the end in mind. As a business person you need to have a plan, know where your business is headed, how you are going to get there and of course, any obstacles you may face along the way.

The main advantage of having a plan is that you can consider all the possibilities available to you. You can look at the opportunities, and set yourself some clear goals. But to be honest, the key to good planning is taking the action.

Marketing Expert, Hannah McNamara: "You need to have an end point to it, something you've got to work towards, whether you call it a goal, an outcome, an objective, or a target. You need to know what you would like to achieve."

"Interestingly enough," she continued, referring to a personal experience, "I spoke to somebody who was an author when I was putting my own book together and she said she had a lot of people including close friends who were going to put a book together on marketing for coaches. She said, 'I'm going to give you help on this as I know you'll do it. They've been talking about it for years.' So I set myself short, sometimes barely achievable goals for things to avoid running out of steam."

Creating your business vision and mission

'Vision without action is a dream. Action without vision is simply passing the time. Action with vision is making a positive difference.' – Joel Barker

Many coaches who are not successful do not have a clear vision. They make short-term plans and frequently change direction rather than make their business work. As you will have found out earlier it makes sense to do a few things well rather than many things badly.

All of the coaches I interviewed for this book have some kind of business vision. Most have a five year plan, broken down into individual projects.

On this subject Women's Business Coach, Allison Marlowe says: "People generally over estimate what they can do in a year and underestimate what they can do in three years." Having your vision will give you a clearer direction to work towards.

If you have a niche, and I hope by now you will have considered this carefully, the next place to start is to develop your vision for your business. A vision can be defined as a statement, which usually consists of a couple of sentences or a paragraph that encapsulates the future that you would like to create for your business. The next step is to create your business mission which is simply who you are and what you do. Most organisations consider their values, so if you haven't already completed the exercise in Chapter 3, I would advise you to do this now.

Defining your business goals

'A goal is a dream with a deadline.' – Napoleon Hill

Once you have your mission statement and an idea of how you would like your business to grow, it is time to develop your business plan and goals. If you are seeking finance from a financial organisation, you will need to have a business plan. But in any case, it is a great working document to have about your business. I must stress that it is a working document and needs to be reviewed and updated regularly in line with your business development.

So what sort of goals or plans might you have for your business? Well, these may be finance-related, as after all, you are running a business. You may have a business growth plan or an exit strategy if you would like to sell your business sometime in the future.

The main rules of planning are:

- Like goals, your plan is written down.
- Review your plan regularly and make adjustments as required.
- Make sure that your goals are SMART – i.e. Specific, Measurable, Achievable, Realistic and Relevant and Time bound – and stated in the present tense.
- They are positively stated, focusing towards what you want rather than away from what you don't want.
- You have clear steps on how to reach your goals.

Strategies for planning

'Organising is what you do before you do something, so that when you do it, it is not all mixed up.' – AA Milne

When you are planning you may find that you are not a natural left-brained person who is logical, structured, likes list writing and likes to prepare carefully. You may have a preference to right-brained planning, which is more visual, liking to see things from different perspectives rather than in a linear way.

Let's hear from my models and their preferred ways of planning.

Gladeana McMahon is a very creative person. For her she finds that using visualisation techniques are a great way to focus on the future. An extremely visual person, Gladeana told me that she visualises everything in technicolour. So if you prefer not to plan in a linear way, take some time to visualise what you want to see in your future business. Sports psychologists help successful athletes to use visualisation to enable them to create the right internal, external or mental state in which to engage in their sport. Whether this is an image of winning a gold medal or breaking a personal best, the aim is to achieve a state of flow. This is an internal state that energises and aligns emotions with the task in hand. The brain, when it creates an image (whether real or imaginary), gives rise to emotional states that will evoke behaviour. Changing the way you think will change the way you feel and, therefore, change the way you behave.

Another way of creating your future visually is to create a vision board of what you want to see in your future business. Simply take a large piece of card and paste images, phrases and words on to the card to represent the goals and objectives you would like to fulfil in your future.

If neither of these tools works for you, there are various other planning activities you can try. Women's Business Coach, Allison Marlowe, like other models, tends to use mind mapping as a planning tool. A mind map, which is a concept introduced by Tony Buzan, is a diagram used to represent words, ideas, tasks, or other items linked to and arranged around a central key word or idea. It is a means of representing topics, ideas, projects, tasks, and similar items in a visual format.

"I like to have a packet of colours to work with when I mind map," said Allison. "I have something in the middle (of the page), for example, this free report, and then I would have the different areas and I'd choose a different colour for each area because it just makes it very clear to me and I can look at it very quickly and focus." Allison strongly believes that successful people take immediate action. "Planning for me quite often comes after a coaching session with one of my coaches. I literally can just put the phone down and get my pad and pens out. So the thought must have come from the coaching and must have just clicked like a light bulb coming on and maybe I would like to describe that as clarity. It's very difficult to analyse because it happens so quickly."

Marketing Coach Hannah McNamara is another person who loves mind maps. "I use mind maps and I use post-it notes," she says. "I've got teeny tiny post-it notes and big ones as well. If I'm running a teleseminar, I'll mind map it and think about the introduction, what am I going to have off there? How long do I need to spend on that? Which is the next topic? I'll mind map it and then I'll do a tidy one to present from. I find it easier to do that than present from a list."

Leadership Coach Duncan Brodie recommended using MindMeister, which is an online mind-mapping and brainstorming tool, as it gives you a structure of what to do, for example, when planning a speaking engagement.

Going back to Hannah's preferences, she also likes to be organised and showed me how she likes to plan on a daily basis. "There is quite a lot of planning that goes on in my head when it is something that's got a definite date," she said. "I then just break it down until I'm left with a 'to do' list." During our interview, Hannah showed me her diary. "I purposely bought this diary," she said, "because it's got appointments down this side and notes down this side. And so I have my to do list every single day and when it's things in advance, like a deadline, that will go in the diary later so that when I open my diary on that day, I know I've got to get that finished today."

Gladeana McMahon talked to me further about planning. "There are many great coaches who should not touch self-employment with a barge pole," she said. "They haven't really got that discipline because you have to get up, you have to make it happen. I've got lots of people now, and I pay lots of people now. But I didn't used to have them. I used to have to type all my letters (and in those days it was letters), I had to run all my administration and I had to get my bring-forward box (this was before the computer), and there was nobody to say start work at 9 a.m. and finish at this time. I had to make sure I got up and when the knock-backs came, and they will, I had to build myself up again. I had my supervisor because originally in therapy you always have a counselling supervisor as someone to talk to about your cases, but when you are a self-employed person with people coming to you, you don't have colleagues, and you have got to be pretty resilient actually. I think you need all of those skills.

"You need to be able to plan, and that is the other thing, you need to have some kind of idea where you are going. What do you want at the end? How will you make this happen? What is the vision? And you need to have time management and stress management skills. You need to take care of yourself as it is very easy to keep on working or not get your pricing policy right so you end up seeing more people than you really should be seeing, but you don't like to turn them down."

Eating your frog

'The secret of getting things done is to act.' – Dante Alighieri

With regards to planning, Allison Marlowe recommends 'eating your frog' as characterised in Brian Tracy's book of the same name. The concept of 'eating your frog' is a metaphor for tackling the most challenging task of the day and the one that you are most likely to put off, but is also likely to be one that will have a positive impact on your life. In Brian Tracy's book, he talks about the vital rules of effective personal time management of decision, discipline and determination.

"It's about eating your frog every single day," said Allison. "Some days the frogs are quite tasty and sometimes they're not tasty. It's about knowing you have to take those steps and having perseverance and determination. I just think those are key qualities that you need to be able to run a successful business." She explains further: "It is also about eating the right frog! You need to know specifically which frog will generate the desired result you require. Implementation is key."

When you have a plan, it is also useful that you review your progress. Suparna Dhar spoke about her successes: "I measure success by the fact that I have been in business for coming up to 3 years and I've met my business plan. I need to manage my costs as I find my costs spiral out of control but is it successful? Yes, but there is room for improvement."

Getting your systems in place

'Expect the best, plan for the worst, and prepare to be surprised.' – Denis Waitley

In relation to having a plan and reviewing its effectiveness, Duncan Brodie said: "I also think it is important to have some sort of performance management system for your business, which is one of the things I've got from Stacey Barr. She does a brilliant little e-book on KPIs (Key Performance Indicators) for small businesses, and one of the things she talks about is a simple scoreboard, but what I've got is a simple spreadsheet and I monitor things like product sales, one-to-one income, my group work, website visits, times on website, all those kind of things. Having the measurement in place and doing that as a routine is important."

Having some sort of system for measurement is important for many of my models, whether this is a simple spreadsheet or a piece of software.

Taking time to prioritise

'A good plan today is better than a perfect plan tomorrow.'
– Proverb

When it comes to planning, it is important to focus on one thing at a time. For example, if you offer multiple products or services, concentrate on marketing each one at a time. Otherwise you will confuse your potential clients as they will find it hard to understand what you do and therefore will be more reluctant to buy from you. In addition, it enables you to maintain your focus and streamline your activities.

There are many tools that can help you to prioritise. One of the most famous was developed by Stephen Covey and outlined in his book, *'The Seven Habits of Highly Effective People'*. The tool he talks about is the time management matrix. To prioritise using this tool, the first thing you need to do is to take a large sheet of paper and divide it into 4 quadrants. Label each quadrant as follows – 1. Urgent and Important, 2. Not Urgent and Important, 3. Urgent and Not Important and 4. Not Urgent and Not Important.

- 'Urgent and important' are the things you need to do now such as emergencies and items with a tight deadline.
- 'Not urgent and important' are the things you plan to do, such as research, scheduling, strategic actions.
- 'Urgent and not important' are those activities which are routine and potential trivia.
- 'Not urgent and not important' are those which are non-productive, such as surfing the internet and reading irrelevant material.

Allocate your tasks to each box. Consider the consequences of doing or not doing something. This will help you to evaluate the significance of the most important tasks. This judgement is crucial for good time management, and once you know what activities are essential for success, you can start working on them. Most inexperienced people, and people who are not good at time management, or in managing their environment, tend to spend most of their time in boxes 1 and 3. Any spare time is typically spent in box 4, which comprises of aimless and non-productive activities. Most people spend the least time of all in box 2, which is the most critical area for strategy and for developing a successful coaching business.

"I write lots of lists," says Suparna Dhar. "I prioritise – I have my Blackberry. I do a lot of planning in terms of the year and breaking it down into school terms, and having check lists. I find that I'm at my best when I'm not stressed; it goes back to that feeling of being centred and controlled and having clear thinking space."

As a further thought, when you are prioritising your activities and planning your time, the most important is to consider the impact of everything you do against your wider goals or aims.

NLP exercise – creating a well formed outcome

This is a great opportunity now to introduce you to a set of questions which make up the NLP technique: 'well formed outcomes'.

'Well formed outcomes' is a term used in NLP to describe a process of defining and refining your goals. Similar to setting 'SMART' goals, it helps you to define the outcome you want to achieve and focus on what you actually want to achieve rather than what you don't want. The technique is made up of a set of 13 questions with the last ones named 'Cartesian Co-ordinates' which are designed to challenge your thinking and make the subconscious work hard!

To start this exercise, take your goal or outcome and apply the following questions to the goal.

1. What do you want? (State in positive terms.)

2. How will you know when you've got it? What will you see, hear, feel, taste?

3. Where, when and with whom do you want this?

4. Where, when and with whom do you NOT want this?

5. What resources do you need to get this?

6. What will happen when you get this?

7. How will getting this benefit you?

8. Do you want this change in any other situation?

9. How will making this change affect other aspects of your life?

Cartesian co-ordinates

What would happen if you did make that change?

What would happen if you didn't make that change?

What wouldn't happen if you did make that change?

What wouldn't happen if you didn't make that change?

Great, you now have an outcome and can plan for the next step which is to become 'work in progress'.

Chapter 10 –
Step 8 Become work in progress

'Success is not the key to happiness. Happiness is the key to success. If you love what you are doing, you will be successful.' – Albert Schweitzer

As a coach, you will have spent time on your personal development to become qualified, and this is not something that can stop there. You may find that there are skills you need to learn to be able to run your business effectively and you may also wish to upgrade your skills so that you can be ahead of the competition.

Coaching training

'When the student is ready, the master appears.'
– Buddhist Proverb

If you haven't already completed your coaching qualification, this is probably a good place to start. You may wish to consider one of the training qualifications accredited by one of the coaching bodies (detailed in the next section). There are a range of options available to you, from distance learning training through organisations such as Newcastle College, to options which include face-to-face training, including The Coaching Academy, Noble Manhattan, Coach-U, Achievement Specialists, Coaches Training Institute (CTI) and the Smart School of Coaching. For most of these options, the training generally includes a practical assessment, written work and other forms of assessment.

In addition, you may also wish to consider a post-graduate certification, for example through any of the following organisations: the Academy of Executive Coaching (AoEC), the i-Coach Academy, Oxford Brookes University, Sheffield Business School or Performance Coach Training and the University of Portsmouth. Please note that these lists are not exhaustive.

Joining a coaching body

'Learning is a treasure that will follow its owner everywhere.'
– Chinese Proverb

Although there is no single recognised body for coaching in the UK, there are organisations that can help you to achieve recognition as a coach.

One of the model coaches that I interviewed is Gladeana McMahon who is the UK Chair of the Association for Coaching (AC). A not for profit organisation, the AC aims to promote best practice, and raise awareness and standards across the coaching industry worldwide.

Advantages of joining organisations such as the AC are that you go through a stringent membership accreditation process to ensure you meet their standards of qualification and practice. This will build your credibility as a coach in your field.

Once a member, renewable yearly, you will have the opportunity to keep up to date on latest coaching developments, receive a regular magazine and support through co-coaching meetings UK-wide, take advantage of online forums, ongoing training and development opportunities and attend an annual conference. In addition, AC members can promote their services through the AC's online directory.

As a member of the AC, I can only comment personally

on the structures implemented by this organisation. There are other coaching bodies that you may also consider joining including the International Institute of Coaching (IIC) (originally the ECI), the European Mentoring and Coaching Council (EMCC) and the International Coach Federation (ICF).

In addition, should you coach in a particular profession, you may wish to be a member of one of their professional bodies. Examples include the Chartered Institute of Personnel and Development or the Chartered Institute of Marketing.

Continuous professional development

'Coaching is 90% attitude and 10% technique.' – Author unknown

Once you have completed your coaching training, there are a range of ongoing development opportunities. As a coach, I believe it is important to plan how you are going to develop your skills further to become more effective.

One of the options available to you is Neuro Linguistic Programming (NLP) training. This could be in the form of a diploma, training for which is usually a couple of days (such as the free course offered by Training Excellence at www.free-nlp.co.uk), or an NLP Practitioner qualification (7-14 days' training) followed by an NLP Master Practitioner qualification which tends to be 14 days plus. Again, like coaching qualifications, there is no recognised awarding body, so if you choose this option, talk to other people who have had training, and ask for their recommendations.

There are a range of other learning opportunities such as signing up for teleseminars, webinars and newsletters as well as learning from others who are experts in your chosen area; I will touch on this shortly. Leadership Coach, Duncan Brodie makes this point: "One of the other things I do is read books from people who are successful in completely unrelated stuff. I am re-reading Duncan Bannatyne's book at the moment (Anyone Can Do It: My Story), and I would recommend it to anybody. I've read James Caan's book, Theo Pathetis' book, Peter Jones' book. I would recommend them all. They are all willing to take balanced risks; they have the hunger, the desire, the self-belief and all the characteristics that are important to run a business."

Hannah McNamara: "I tend to listen to things on my IPod – that's the way I learn." She added a caveat though. "I take a lot of things in and used to think that it must be true if somebody's said it or they've written an e-book on it. But now, I think a bit more and am more critical of things I read and hear."

Having room to grow

'Man's mind, once stretched by a new idea, never regains its original dimensions.' – Oliver Wendell Holmes

As you are 'work in progress', there is room for you to grow, both in terms of your own skills and in terms of your business and success.

"I offer a blend of coaching and mentoring," said Allison Marlowe. "I would say that I am successful. However, I would also say that there is room for expansion, room to grow, and I see myself as many other business women out there. It's like another journey and I wouldn't expect to be successful straight away and I can honestly say, hand on heart, that it took two and a half years before I reaped the benefits of everything that I was putting into place there.

"I'm constantly learning more, and the more I learn I discover there is even more to learn. We live in a fast-paced ever changing society – so it's important to keep up with the changes. Even in marketing there have been huge changes in the past five years. Just look at social media as an example."

Suzy Greaves: "I read a lot of self-help books which helps me to get into different mindsets; I like to learn from the masters. I don't feel like I'm done yet. I feel like I'm just a beginner in this ongoing learning, and I am committed to achieving excellence and growth."

Who supports the coach?

'The purpose of learning is growth, and our minds, unlike our bodies, can continue growing as we continue to live.' – Mortimer Adler

Another consideration as a coach is who supports you? There are many options available. I personally believe that we are all 'work in progress' and in doing so, need additional support ourselves. I have a business coach and mentor and a supervisor, both of whom are important in my own ongoing effectiveness and personal development.

The advantages of having a coach are that he or she will support you with your ongoing personal development in whichever areas are required. Usually non-directional in their approach, a coach will enable you to improve your performance or skills.

You may choose instead to have a mentor who will be able to guide you further, and the advantages are that this person will have experience in the field you would like to develop. For example, if you want to develop your business, a business mentor will be able to guide you, provide you with ideas, strategies and information to help you to develop your business further.

Supercoach Michael Neill told me that in his view it is essential that all coaches have their own coach. "I am amazed at how many coaches don't have a coach," he said. "It's like, what do you think coaching is for? They say, 'OK, I'm doing quite well now, I don't need a coach anymore,' but coaching isn't just for when you're *not* doing quite well. If you can't overcome your own objections to spending money on a coach, how are you ever going to overcome your client's objections? If you can't convince yourself that it is worth investing money on coaching, you are going to struggle with any integrity to convince your potential clients. I generally have two, sometimes three coaches going at any one time, covering different things with different coaches. There hasn't been a time in my business when I haven't had a regular coach as well as mentors and peer support."

Supervisors have for a long time been an important part of the counselling profession and are becoming of increasing importance within coaching as well. Supervision is a formal arrangement which allows a coach to spend time with a qualified professional to reflect on their work with clients. It is a confidential and non-judgemental space for the coach to discuss areas of concern or issues with their supervisor. It also enables the coach to maintain their personal standards and ethics, by being able to explore issues with that professional.

One of the issues that many coaches may face, especially during the first few years of their practice is that clients will metaphorically hold up a mirror in front of the coach. Suzy Greaves gave me an example of when it happened to her. "I once turned down a client because she had many miscarriages," she said, "and I had had a few miscarriages before and I couldn't help that client when I was pregnant. I find it fascinating. Every client I get is a mirror of me past, present or future and I think, 'Oh no, I can't believe it!' It is about accepting all of those parts of yourself."

There may be times when you need to turn down work or share experiences with a supervisor to make sure that it doesn't affect you in the longer term.

All of the coaches I interviewed had some form of coaching, mentoring, supervision, and some had all three. Big Leap Coach, Suzy Greaves, told me that she always has a coach, and Parent Coach, Suparna Dhar, talked to me about the importance of her ongoing development and part of that is through having supervision.

Modelling excellence

'Never become so much of an expert that you stop gaining expertise. View life as a continuous learning experience.' – Denis Waitley

The aim of my research for this book was to enable me to model excellence in respect to coaches who are already successful in this field. This is a great concept to follow when developing your own coaching business. However, one thing I have learnt is that it is important to be individual. Although you can learn the strategies that successful coaches use, it is important to develop your own unique style.

Earlier on in the book, Women's Business Coach, Allison Marlowe told me that she invests in her own development. To this she added: "I'm a great believer in learning from other people, people that I see as successful, and modelling their success. But what I would like to say about that is that I do invest an awful lot on learning. Having the skills and the knowledge is one thing but the real key to success is taking the action. It's actually putting that into action and taking that next step. I think we can all learn new skills, new things. So that's the journey that I'm still on and I would say that I am now on the next chapter of the journey. And that journey has had its successes and it has had its challenges."

Suzy Greaves: "You need to be yourself and to be comfortable in your own skin. It's also about knowing your strengths and knowing your weaknesses and embracing both of them. We all bring something to the party."

So learning is one thing, but being authentic and taking action is essential in order to build and create a successful business.

Stepping out of your comfort zone

'Move out of your comfort zone. You can only grow if you

are willing to feel awkward and uncomfortable when you try something new.' – Brian Tracy

When it comes to action, what many of you will do is to step out of your comfort zone. Your comfort zone refers to an environment with which you are comfortable, and without risk. Successful business people are those who routinely step out of their comfort zones to accomplish their goals and desires.

"You can only have the experience if you put yourself in those situations," said Executive Coach, Blaire Palmer. "Confidence doesn't come before the action; confidence comes as a result of the action. You have to take the action first. If you hate networking, you've got to get out there and network. If you hate talking to people, talk to people. If you hate going into big buildings and dressing up in corporate gear, buy yourself some flash corporate gear and go into big buildings. And you will feel better in time. Your comfort zone expands. Continue to go out.

"Your comfort zone is that place that feels safe, but it is not necessarily the place where you are going to create and develop your business. Sometimes it takes that move out of your comfort zone to allow yourself to reinforce your new beliefs. If you don't like networking, but you go along to a new group, meet some influential contacts or even pick up a new piece of business, it will reinforce your belief that you can do that."

The comfort zone – anonymous

I used to have a comfort zone
where I knew I couldn't fail,
The same four walls of busy work
were really more like a jail.

I longed so much to do the things
I'd never done before,
But I stayed inside my comfort zone
and paced the same old floor.

I said it didn't matter
that I wasn't doing much,
I said I didn't care for things
like diamonds or furs and such.

I claimed to be so busy
with the things inside my zone,
But deep inside I longed for
something special of my own.

I couldn't let my life go by
just watching others win,
I held my breath and stepped outside
to let the change begin.

I took a step and with new strength
I'd never felt before,
I kissed my comfort zone good bye
and closed and locked the door.

If you are in a comfort zone,
afraid to venture out,
Remember that all winners
were at one time filled with doubt.

A step or two and words of praise
can make your dreams come true.
Greet your future with a smile,
success is there for you!

NLP exercise – creating a future time line

The purpose of this exercise is to create your own personal time line or vision of your future, allowing you to define how you are going to reach your future business vision. There are various forms of time line interventions – this exercise is not a traditional way of time line work but a spatial way of goal setting. This is designed as being a simple exercise to allow you to fine tune your own personal and business development goals.

1. Take a business development goal and ask yourself the following question: When you have achieved your goal, what will you see, hear and feel? Ask yourself what is important to you about achieving this.

2. Working with a partner, create an imaginary line on the floor in front of you, which represents your future time line, ensuring you have plenty of space.

3. Walk along the time line into your future, where your goal is situated. Associate yourself into the experience of having achieved your outcome, what you feel, hear and see. Allow that feeling of success and accomplishment to intensify.

4. Turn around and look back towards the present. Notice what steps are required to achieve this outcome, and with your partner writing down your thoughts, state what you need to do to achieve this outcome, planning back from the future to the present position.

5. Once you have done this, go back to the present position and notice any other steps or tweaks you need to make.

This will help you to programme the planning into your mind and get into action to take the first step. You may also wish to walk beyond your goal into the future and turn around and notice all the wonderful things that have happened to achieve your goal. When you walk back to the present, you will also feel an automatic pull towards your goal.

Well we are just moving on to the final two steps to transform your coaching practice, and through the tools, tips and exercises, you should be developing a great action plan to work towards. Take a few moments to note your key insights before moving on to the next stage to develop a winning mindset.

Chapter 11 –
Step 9 Develop a winning mindset

'Our deepest fear is not that we are inadequate. Our deepest fear is that we are powerful beyond measure. It is our light, not our darkness that most frightens us. We ask ourselves, who am I to be brilliant, gorgeous, talented, fabulous? Actually, who are you not to be?' – Marianne Williamson

One of the themes that came out of interviewing the model coaches is that you need a strong self-belief to run a successful business. But it came down to more than that; it is also about developing a mindset for success.

A mindset is a way of thinking or a state of mind, and ultimately it affects the way that you think and how successful you are. The NLP techniques outlined in this book aim to help you to develop this success and also to reprogramme your mind to give you the edge.

When you have a winning mindset, you will know what you do well and will do more of it. You will be a great coach and will be constantly developing your skills. Just as importantly, you will confidently believe in yourself and your abilities.

I asked Blaire Palmer about her own mindset. "I believe that if you believe a thing is possible, you find a way to make it work, to make it happen," she said. "I believe we are more capable than we believe we are capable. I like the Marianne Williamson quote – the one that Nelson Mandela used. It's the fear we are powerful beyond measure that stops us. But only by being true to ourselves do we inspire others to be the same. I believe that. I try to be as genuine as I can.

"I really believe in the work that I do, I believe that work can be meaningful, whatever work that you do. I think that companies can operate profitably and care about people, the people who work for them, and the people who buy their products, their clients and other stakeholders. I believe people are capable of change, of shifting their mindset. One of the main reasons I do my work is that I find it tragic that many people tolerate or even hate their job. They hate the company they work for, the commute, the people they work for, and it's such a tragic waste. They get home exhausted, go to bed and do the same the next day. But it is possible to make a difference."

How to have what you want rather than what you don't want

'Happiness is not having what you want. It is wanting what you have.' – Rabbi Hyman Schachtel

What every great coach knows is that you need to focus on what you want rather than what you don't want and focus on your outcomes. That is to say, instead of focusing on what you *don't* want, ask yourself what you *do* want instead. Once you have a clear idea of what you do want and what your plan for your business is, it will make it easier to achieve. Phrase your goals positively and also reward yourself for what you have achieved. Having a written record of these victories can be a great motivator when something has not gone to plan.

If you set yourself a negative goal it focuses you in the wrong direction. When it is positive it focuses your attention on what you need to do to make it happen. The subconscious mind does not process negatives so if I said: 'Don't think of a pink elephant,' what has just happened? I bet you just imagined a pink elephant! So having a positive intent reinforces empowering thought processes.

To get more of what you want, watch what you say, how you say things and the impact of your thoughts.

When you know what you want, write it down and put it somewhere you will see every day.

Who is your role model?

'Having a role model in life is a great thing to have; one who provides us with direction and inspiration. However, we will forever be restricted by that person's limitations if we live within their boundaries. Be influenced, but set your own standards and develop your own principles, if you are ever to live beyond someone else's dreams.' – Jason Shahan

Although I mentioned earlier that it is important that you retain your identity when becoming a successful business person, I do believe that role models can have a powerful influence.

Who inspires you?

Follow these people and take on board what they do and also learn from their mistakes. You will be able to learn what they do well and how you can do something similar.

Hannah McNamara has her own role models. "I want to learn from people I can see, warts and all," she said. "If I'm going to look up to somebody I need to know all the other things that are going on, when they make their mistakes, what they've done that they've learnt from, things they would do differently. Not just that they've digested a few self-help books and are going to regurgitate it now."

Why businesses fail

'It is hard to fail, but it is worse never to have tried to succeed.' – Theodore Roosevelt

Statistics in the UK state that 25% of businesses fail in their very first year and only 20% make it to their sixth birthday. The experts I interviewed for this book have been in business for somewhere between three and twenty plus years.

Businesses tend to fail because of any of the following reasons:

- The business is not commercially viable; although a business does not need to be unique, there needs to be a market for a product or service.
- The owner spends more money than the business earns.
- The business owner waits for everything to be perfect before taking action; although planning is important, it is important to try things out to see if something works, then learn from this action.
- Lack of preparation or planning; although action is important, planning is equally essential.
- Weak marketing or influencing skills; if these are not your strong points, learn what is needed or outsource this to an expert.

Women's Business Coach, Allison Marlowe has written a report about why businesses fail. "The reasons are there," she says. "It is lack of research – people not really doing their research. They don't really understand what it is that their clients want, so you need to sell them what they want and give them what they need to make it a viable business. Also they may find they have a lack of direction, or feel isolated. These are all reasons why people tend to give up and I think it is so easy to give up if you don't have that mindset."

In terms of running a successful coaching business, Steve Marriott said: "Coaching is something you absolutely have to want to do. You can do or be anything you want to be, but you've got to want to help. Some people get confused as to the end goal, and for me the end goal is actually doing the coaching. Some people get carried away with the 'romantic' side, such as wanting to emulate people who are earning a large amount of money, rather than being the best coach they can be, and living the values they aspire to."

Make sure your 'why' is big enough

'One of the things that may get in the way of people being lifelong learners is that they're not in touch with their passion. If you're passionate about what it is you do, then you're going to be looking for everything you can to get better at it.' – Jack Canfield

If you have followed the other steps in this book, you are well on your way to success. However, if you are wondering whether you have made the right decision to run your own business or perhaps things are not quite going to plan, you may need to reconnect with developing a positive mindset.

If you are going to be successful, you need to make sure your 'why' is big enough. Your 'why' is the reason you became a coach and set up your business in the first place. It is your dream or your goal, and the reason you want to do this is to bring yourself a sense of fulfilment and accomplishment. It is the motivation for you to get off your backside and take action. So this means that your 'why' needs to be big enough for you to take action and if your 'why' *is* big enough, the 'how' will come.

In my interview with Steve Marriott he spoke about the six human needs that Anthony Robbins[3] mentions in his 'Unleash the Power Within' event.

To summarise, there are six universal human needs and the order of importance differs for different people and these needs are linked to our beliefs. The six needs are:

- Certainty – this relates to people wanting comfort and certainty in their lives, which comes from having control.

3 Anthony Robbins is a leading US coach, entrepreneur and author – see 'Further resources' to find out more or go to www.tonyrobbins.com.

- Uncertainty – at the same time as wanting certainty, people also want variety, challenges, and new goals.
- Significance – people want to feel special, unique, important, and for life to have significance.
- Connection and love – people want to be cared for, be part of a community and be loved.
- Growth – many people want to improve their skills, stretch their minds and excel in certain areas.
- Contribution – the desire to contribute towards others and make the world a better place.

Anthony Robbins says that everybody will find that some of these are more important and significant to them. Everything that somebody does will fulfil a need within them. Having an understanding of these needs will make a difference to what you do and how you can support and understand your clients.

Which of these needs are most important to you?

_____

_____

_____

How can you make sure these are reflected in your business?

_____

_____

_____

Hannah McNamara: "You need to make the decision that something's going to work. And then once you've made that decision that something's going to work, you then have to find the path to doing it. Decide what product you are going to produce, think through how that's going to work, how people are going to get the best from it, and then decide when that's going to happen. So I do actually start with the deadline when I want something to be done and then I work back. You work back on your timeline of what leads up to the end point and what the milestones are along the way."

Blaire Palmer spoke about the changes she has made in her business. "I believed when I was pregnant that I could go back to work part time and work less and earn more," she said. "When I came back to work it was during the recession which affected my mindset and the mindset of my clients and I worried that maybe it wasn't possible. But now, two years on, I know it is possible. This year has been the second most financially successful year of my business so far in ten years. It is to do with you. You decide what you want and find ways to make it happen rather than be influenced by what other people have done and believing that's the only way it can be done."

Walking your talk

'Walking your talk is a great way to motivate yourself. No one likes to live a lie. Be honest with yourself, and you will find the motivation to do what you advise others to do.'
– Vince Poscente

To run a successful coaching business, you need to believe in your abilities as a coach. Steve Marriott: "If you are not confident in your ability to get people to their outcomes as a coach then you are limiting your chances of success because you're not allowing people to be confident in you. One critical factor is 'state leads state', and if you go in with a wobble or uncertainty then you're just not allowing your client to have any confidence in you. There has to be a degree of confidence to find the right question. Coaching isn't an exact science, you might ask three questions when you could ask one question, but when you find the right question that's great – like hitting the 'Sweet Spot' on a racket. You can take this person to a different place in their life."

Allison Marlowe agrees that to be successful you need to believe in what you are doing. "You have to walk your talk and you have to believe in what it is that you are doing so that other people can see that it is a genuine, authentic you. This belief has to be so strong; if you aren't able to talk about your product or service with 100% certainty then how can you expect your prospects to believe in you?

"I think that if you want to create that mindset, you have to start with yourself. It is my belief, but I think personal development is crucial to all parts of life. And I think that if you want to be a success at anything, you have to know and understand yourself. And if you look at the Maslow or the NLP hierarchy, the neurological levels are that you have got to understand yourself, your behaviours, if you are going to be successful. And just by understanding yourself, where you are today, doesn't mean that in two years' time you won't be re-evaluating your personal beliefs then. It's just life-long learning, isn't it?"

I asked Dawn Breslin what sort of mindset she needs to run her business successfully. "I've just come across Roger Hamilton, Wealth Dynamics," she replied. "He has written a book called *Your Life, Your Legacy*, and he identifies the different characters that are necessary within a business. I think I have an advantage within my own character; I am creative and have dynamo energy. When I get an idea, I run at it. Seeds are planted and half way up before I decide to consider the project. I work from morning to night to get it to happen. I'm not too hard on myself. I don't have the harsh critic that stops me living my potential. I say to myself, 'Go on give it a try Breslin, and do your very best'. If that voice is really judgemental, you're doomed. Or if you haven't got the dynamic energy or the brand consciousness to push out a project, bring somebody on board who has – because that makes a business successful."

I interviewed Suzy Greaves in the autumn of 2009. "I am in the middle of a transition right now," she said. "My first business was to coach people how to change career and how to start their own business. That was what I concentrated on and to great success. I've gone from a really boring job in Yorkshire and trained to be a journalist and trained to be a coach, so I know what it is like and I train lots of people to go through this process. That process is to give yourself a purpose, and live a life that reflects your values. That's what I've done."

"What makes me successful," she says, "is that I am a naturally enthusiastic person – I genuinely champion people. It's innately being who you are, playing to your natural strengths and letting that shine."

Gladeana McMahon talked to me about kindness. "I do believe in kindness," she said. "I think it was James Joyce who said there are three rules in life: 'be kind, be kind and be kind'. I do believe in that and I think it's really important and if we can just do the small things, they don't have to be big things, just the small things can make life pleasant."

She went on to talk about the 1946 film, *Beautiful Life* with James Stewart. "There is a wonderful film and it's about this guy who lives in a small town in America and he gets very depressed and miserable and he says to himself, 'I don't matter, if I wasn't here, so what?' Anyway, this little angel comes down and although he's still alive, the angel shows him what the world would be like if he wasn't there. Although he is only an ordinary Joe, there are all these people in this little town who have been touched by him, and he sees how their lives are all the poorer because he is not in it and so he gets to see that it's the small things in life that make big differences. You can't tell that an act of kindness might not make a difference to someone. You can't; you don't know what the chain of events is going to be."

Looking after your inner needs

'Our sense of worth, of well-being, even our sanity depends upon our remembering. But, alas, our sense of worth, our well-being, our sanity also depends upon our forgetting.' – Joyce Appleby

One of the things I have come across many times in running my business is the importance of looking after my own needs. Although you may want to run a successful coaching business, you have to look after your own needs first. You can work sixteen hours a day, seven days a week, which is great and may be necessary at times, but it isn't conducive to looking after your own needs. And if you don't look after yourself, how can you look after anyone else?

This is a topic that was raised by many of the models. To develop their business they have had to make sacrifices in their lives, put in long hours, but some have learnt the hard way and have now put in strategies to allow them to take time out and not face burn-out too.

Dawn Breslin has a tendency to work long days. "My job is my life, it's a vocation; it's not just a job" she said. "Some weeks I work every single night and I work twelve to fifteen hours a day and you do that when you love something." I asked her how she recognises when she needs to rebuild her energy. "I'm still learning," she admitted. "The problem with having dynamo energy is that at times my brain can't compute and sometimes I end up in a heap. I don't always clock in before the energy goes, then I'm 'rebalancing' in my hot tub at the end of the garden, and I know how to do that really effectively."

Suzy Greaves had a similar point of view: "I have a theory about characters from Winnie the Pooh. There is something about Winnie the Pooh; some people are Piglet and a bit fearful and I am Tigger. You know bouncing and I do get tired and it's about looking after your energy and not doing anything. But you get the energy from doing things you love so the more you are in the big place, the more energy you've got."

Hannah McNamara found that to get her business off the ground, she had to put long hours in. However, she also found that her work/life balance was getting ridiculous. "I was getting up at 7 a.m.," she said, "starting work on the computer before I had even got dressed and finishing at 11 o'clock at night." So she took an office with her business partner to allow her to get her life back in balance.

Both Allison Marlowe and Suparna Dhar also have strategies when they need to focus on themselves. Allison states how important it is for her to get back to nature when she has lost clarity or focus. One of her favourite things to do is to go and sit on a hill with a 360 degree view. Suparna says that she loves to go for walks by the river and take time to enjoy it.

Staying motivated

'To accomplish great things, we must not only act, but also dream; not only plan, but also believe.' – Anatole France

For other people, it might not be the work/life balance that is a problem, but the difficulty in staying motivated to get their business on track. Most of my models demonstrated an internal motivation to develop and advance their business.

Suzy Greaves measures her success on a feeling of motivation. "I used to define success in terms of external money," she said. "For my business to run, I would need to earn a minimum of £3000 a month and work less than thirty hours a week. That was my version of success. But now, I think I am measuring it more on a sense of whether I feel excited by my work, whether I feel motivated to get up in the morning. Do I feel excited about my work? – Yes I do!"

Gladeana McMahon has a huge amount of internal motivation. "Part of motivating myself is having a picture," she states. "My in-trays over there for example, everything is in a plastic wallet and everything is there that I need. So if I had a lot of stuff on my desk that I was sorting through, then, what I would do is create an image of having it all nicely in the right tray, all filed away. This image is my motivator because I know I will feel good when it's like this." She has pictures running in her head all the time, and when I asked her more about these she said: "Many of them are of people doing things, and they are like running movies – a constant stream of movies. So if somebody rings me up and tells me that tomorrow I'm going to do a presentation in the afternoon, I would visualise that presentation. I may never have been to the venue but I'll have an image in my mind about it so I'll be quite excited about going and doing it. The same applies to clients, imagining them doing things that they are trying to achieve and what that would look like."

Women's Business Coach, Allison Marlowe: "When I wake in the morning, I actually feel excited. I will often feel bubbles in my stomach when I feel excited. There are two ways to describe it. One is like the fizz in a lemonade bottle – I have to be careful with that as it can explode sometimes. But the other is more of a gentle feeling, which is how I would describe the waking up in the morning feeling. It is like someone is waving bubbles very gently, like a children's pot of bubbles."

Living your passions

'The way to get started is to quit talking and begin doing.' – Walt Disney

Brian Tracy, in his popular CD set, Success Mastery Academy, says this about starting a new business:

"The key is getting into a new business, product or service you are passionate about. You love it! That is so important to you that you cannot stop thinking about it or talking about it. You love to use it and would sell it to your mother, your father, your sister, your brother ... It's a good test. Can you sell it to your mother? Can you sell it to your brother? Can you sell it to your best friend? Can you sell it to your co-workers? Can you talk about it so confidently and passionately to anybody? If you feel reluctant, or uneasy or tense talking about it to the people you know closely, I can guarantee that you will never be successful selling it to people you don't know at all.

"Many people get into businesses because they think they are going to make a lot of money. That is exactly the wrong reason for getting into a business – because you will fail. You must get into a business of any kind because you love it – you are in love with the business – you love the product; I mean you are on fire with it. If you only do it for the money, what we have found is that as soon as you hit the wall, which you will, you will collapse. You will not have enough energy to stick to it when things get rough. But if you live it, you will keep going; you will be like the energiser bunny, just keep going and going and going. So it is very important that you have that commitment."

My thanks go to Brian Tracy for allowing me to publish this quote. Please see Chapter 3 for his biography or go to www.briantracy.com.

As the developer of 'Consciously Female', Dawn Breslin considers herself to be a teacher rather than a coach. When I visited Dawn in her lovely home just outside Edinburgh, the space exuded a feeling of spirituality and calmness.

Dawn works with groups of women for an eight week course at her home where she teaches them to find their passions. "I start off with somebody who comes along and I talk about people being like onions," she said. "At the core of the onion you've got this pot of potential and then you have these layers. My first job is to get to *who* you really are, and your passion and your potential; you have to get rid of the layers. You've got to learn to let go of the past, you've got to learn to let go of things that have hurt you, and you've got to get to your purest self. Then we get to your essence and everybody's essence is different. At the core there is something there that is unique and uniquely you. Then I spend time aligning you to be passionate about your daily life, from when you get up in the morning, make conscious choices. Once we get to who you are and your light shines, we position you on track, taking baby steps to help you to get to know who you are. It's knowing what excites you and interests you, and having the energy to do all that." When she has this energy and is in the zone, she feels so excited! "I'm excitable and in that place everything is effortless," she says.

When Suparna Dhar is in a peak state, she says to herself, 'You can do it. You have the confidence, and go with the flow'. She went onto tell me: "I love this thing about saying be fearless, I love it. I have a buzziness, a certain energy, I feel grounded so that I know where I want to go." This state affects her physiology, the feelings in her stomach and her focus on her own successes and those of her clients.

Gladeana McMahon had this to say about her own positive mindset: "Well, not only does it make life much more fun, but I think it makes you more successful. Let's be fair, you'll attract people to you, you're going to do more, take more risks so how can that not be positive and bring goodies to you."

Maintaining your confidence

'Make the most of yourself, for that is all there is of you.' – Ralph Waldo Emerson

Another area that links to developing a winning mindset is having and maintaining confidence in yourself.

Allison Marlowe: "When you first learn something, you want to be confident at it and confidence grows over time and the more you replicate it, the easier it becomes. Like learning to drive or learning to ride a bike. I think you can put that analogy to running your business. I can remember when I first coached over the telephone I had to put on my makeup, had to make sure my hair was done and that I was dressed appropriately, but now I just pick up the phone. It was all about feeling the part. As my confidence grew, I didn't feel the need to put on that persona. But now, when I want to do something new, such as putting a video on the website or something, the first time you do it, it's not going to be easy. But if I start doing it on a regular basis, I don't need the same strength of mindset as I know how to do it. But I do need the attitude to make sure it happens. I need the drive, which is very important."

Celebrating your own successes

'People are like stained-glass windows. They sparkle and shine when the sun is out, but when the darkness sets in their true beauty is revealed only if there is light from within.' – Elisabeth Kübler-Ross

When I visited Dawn Breslin, she sent me away with a copy of her book, *Dawn Breslin's Guide to Superconfidence* and a success journal. This leads me on to the next part of developing a winning mindset, and that is to celebrate your own successes. As a coach and business person, you will spend a lot of time with your clients helping them to lead a life they will love, but you need to remember to celebrate your own successes too. One of the ways of doing this is to complete a success journal, recording your achievements every evening before going to bed.

Suparna Dhar told me about how she develops a positive mindset. "I think about all the positive things that have happened to me. At the moment, I'm in a particularly great mindset as things are going my way. When things don't go my way, I have a reflective diary, and I write things that have happened that haven't worked and what I have learnt from them. I also have my law of attraction book and things I have asked for and underneath I have the proof. I have an internal gratefulness section where internally I am grateful and externally, I do things for charity and give to somebody else or another organisation."

NLP Exercise – Behavioural Modelling

Just as I did when I initially started the research for this book, it is important to learn from the people who do what you want to do really well. You can do this by finding out more about what makes these people tick and their experiences, knowledge and expertise and following the suggestions here.

At its simplest, modelling is the study of the thoughts, behaviours, skills, values, beliefs and other qualities that help people to get the results they want to achieve. You can learn more about someone's strategy for doing something and find out more about their model of the world.

You can model other people's behaviour by:

- Being curious.
- Asking questions.
- Listening to their responses and checking your understanding of their responses.
- Paying attention to their non-verbal responses, and the language they use.
- Finding out exactly what they do when they are doing something; this will include a precise description of what, how, when, where and why they do it.

To model someone who does something you want to do really well, find out their strategies. Ask them what they do, how they do it, who they model, and what else works for them. In addition, follow some of the strategies used by the models in this book and the four-step process below.

Step 1 – in which area do you want to excel?

Step 2 – find 3 people who are very successful in this area.

Step 3 – what makes this person different? What are his or her behavioural patterns? How does he or she get results? What does he or she do that is different from people who are not getting results?

Step 4 – make a change and test it.

Now you have learnt how to develop a winning mindset by modelling the experts. Finally, what can we learn from the people who run a successful coaching business? This is revealed in the next chapter.

Chapter 12 –
Step 10 Learn from the experts

I hope, by now, this book has offered you many ideas that you can put into practice. In this chapter, I would like to leave you with the top tips from each of the experts. In Chapter 13 I will talk you through the next steps you can take to create your own successful coaching business.

Allison Marlowe

"One of the tips would be for you to really scrutinise what you believe in and ask yourself some questions around that. Make sure that you do really believe in it. Let me give you an example: When I set up as a parent coach I thought that's what I wanted to do, and I found I didn't. Coaching is what I wanted to do. The area I was coaching in wasn't right. I didn't enjoy it at all. It didn't stretch me, so I think that it is really important to actually look at what it is that you are offering. It needs to reflect your beliefs and your mindset. I think it all starts with you as a person, what you believe in and perhaps what the gaps are. I'm a great believer in modelling in any case so find out what has worked out for other people. That would definitely be a tip. And I think the other thing is that I don't think that anyone should give something up, but I also think that you shouldn't pursue something that isn't going to work. Be able to let things go."

Blaire Palmer

"Take yourself seriously. If you are dipping your toe in

the water or it is sort of a hobby or you feel like you can't make it work – surprise, surprise, it's not going to work! It's always a little bit smaller than you dream of so if you dream really small, it will be even smaller than that. Have you heard of the Robert Browning quote? 'A man's reach should exceed his grasp or what's a heaven for?' I am trying to reach the ceiling; I don't quite reach the ceiling, but if I only knew I could reach here ... aim high... do not scale back your life to fit the business. Make the business fit your life."

Blaire also makes this suggestion: "Be on your own journey of self development. Whatever it is, you must be constantly exposed to being challenged around your beliefs and your assumptions and your fears. Also learn about business. Understand how to keep a business going. Set aside money for your taxes. Also have a book-keeper, Virtual Assistant, and IT person."

Dawn Breslin

"You have to live it yourself, live an inspired life. You can't teach anyone to have it; you can't create it unless you are doing it. So you've got to construct it so that you are oozing out. It is about loving your clients, about healing. I will believe in you, love you, nurture you, direct you to get you to where you want to go. I have got my life in balance which is really important. If you are loaded with baggage, how are you going to teach people? Your space has got to be inspirational.

"Coaching is another transaction, another way of helping. It isn't a sterile process that you take people through, it's two individuals working together; one with experience to direct and guide the other individual. It is nothing to do with the process, just to help you on your way to express your intention and direction. You need to treat your clients with absolute respect. Intuitively go with your client and believe in them, and ... believe in their potential."

Duncan Brodie

"The first thing I would say is actually get some business-building support early on. In hindsight, that is something I should have done from day one. The second thing would be to get yourself sorted out on a niche. It's not to say you can't take anyone else who comes along, but you've got to find a target so you can concentrate your marketing, if nothing else.

"Be completely realistic, as it is going to take you a period of time to get anywhere near the level of income you want. From a standing start, I would say it will take you anything up to a couple of years to get to that point. The other thing I would say is, don't start incurring unnecessary costs; don't have an office just because you think you need to have an office; don't have a book-keeper to do the three invoices a month you are doing. Make sure you are taking care of all the legal stuff, for example, get yourself a business accountant, get yourself registered with the data protection register, and check out whether you have got a liability for business rates if you are working from a home office. You've got to check out all of those things, get your tax and company structure sorted out. The infrastructure stuff has to get sorted out. Finally, give things enough time to see if they are worthwhile. A lot of people do something once and it doesn't work – that's no good. Once you have set out your intention, keep doing it."

Gladeana McMahon

"Look at who you are, what you do already, where you feel you want to go, and how to build on what you have. Teach yourself to trust yourself, and do more of what you're doing right in these situations. Learn what you can take from a situation and put it into another situation. And when you have a knock or whatever, it's ok to go 'Uuurrrrgh!' I do that, acknowledge the negative feeling and then let it dissipate. It's also acknowledging what I am grateful for in my life. What are the wonderful things that I don't notice?

What are the things I can do for others; there is a buzz in helping others. There is a buzz about smiling to someone on the Tube and them smiling back, because they think, 'Isn't it nice to see a smiling face for once on the Tube.' And things like that. And it's contagious. I'd also say laugh every day; I laugh whenever I can. Smile and laugh because it releases happy hormones and it's free and it's legal. I'm a great one for giggling and laughing and finding every appropriate opportunity to do so.

"One more thing – be determined. Do what you love – live your values. Never take yourself too seriously. Do the right things and the right things will follow. And ... have fun."

Hannah McNamara

"Don't keep going to every coaching training thing you can go to, don't get yourself so immersed in the whole personal development world that you can't talk to a normal person. That will not help you get clients. The more you talk about limiting beliefs, gremlins, 'swishing' and all of that, you're just talking gobble-de-gook. Clients do not want to hear about that, they are only interested in themselves and what you can do to help them. And that also means get out and talk to people who are within your target market. I think this is why a lot of coaches end up coaching coaches or being the mentor coach or whatever because they are so deep into that world that they are the only people they connect with.

"Be businesslike and accept that you will need to know more than just your coaching techniques to do this and more than just marketing techniques and you will need to learn about sales, finance, accounts, administration, legal, and insurance. You have to know all about that and if you don't know about it, don't go to a coach who is just going to be non directive. Just go to someone who is an expert in that."

Marian Way

"Spending time with people who know about marketing is a good idea because you're learning from the experts.

There are a lot of marketing programmes and you need to decide what to do and I know I am basing my decision on the relationship I have with the person I'm working with.

"Patience and perseverance are important. It is easy to give up, particularly when you are new."

Michael Neill

"Success does not require a positive mindset, but enjoying success does. If your coaching business is not a part of your wonderful life, what's the point?

"You need to keep your feet moving. Woody Allen said '80% of success is turning up' which I think he may have been underestimating. If you keep showing up and you keep doing it, you're going to get so much further than someone who is confident but only wants to do it on Thursdays.

"I don't believe there is a right way to do things, but what I've seen is that you get the best results when you're doing what you love and want to do. On some of our practice-building sessions we teach thirty-six different ways to market yourself. For each person, there will be two or three of those strategies that really appeals to them. What makes marketing feel like hard work is when you think you are supposed to do it the way someone else does it. I would say do whatever you need to do to get past that. Discover the way you most like to do it and do it that way. Not only will your business begin to thrive, you will have so much more fun building it. Worst case, you're enjoying your life; best case, you're enjoying your life and live in a big house!"

Steve Marriott

"Get absolutely clear for yourself about what it is that you do and the benefits that this brings to people, what you are worth, how much you want to earn, who you want to earn it with, and most importantly, what you won't do.

"Everyone has the resources they need to have what they want. If a person wants something enough, they can have it. The reason people don't have what they want is that something gets in the way of achieving it (usually fear of failure) or they just don't want it enough.

"The key to 'success' is getting people to define what they really want, committing to it, 'getting into the game' (being clear about what's involved to get there) and taking action."

Suparna Dhar

"Remember that there is no such thing as failure, only feedback. Really believe very passionately about positivity. Whatever happens, it's going to have a positive outcome. For me, I think success is somehow linked to someone who is very organised at whatever level, but someone needs to be organised to access information, access things whether that's themselves being organised or paying people to be organised."

Suzy Greaves

"I would say that where I am with the coaching business is that there is a way to make your business work. You've just got to find it. And if you've got that mindset, it's really good. You need to learn some new skills like marketing or how to build a database. Find people who can do that and learn from them. I was very ashamed when my business wasn't working and not working more quickly; it's about a call to action. Go and find out what you need to do to make this work."

NLP Exercise – Believing in your excellence

Thank you to Jenny Heath, www.therelationshippeople.co.uk, for this exercise, which has been adapted for the purposes of this chapter.

The aim of this exercise is to raise awareness of how different states affect our behaviour and how we can influence our state to generate the response we want.

Our behaviour is driven by the state we are in and this is a good exercise for noticing the different states we may be in, in relation to a different circumstance. For this exercise, you will be using the circumstance of business. We will be using spatial anchoring which I mentioned in Chapter 7 as it gives you the chance to choose the state you want to be in.

RUBBISH	GOOD
EXCELLENT	EXPERT

Step 1 – create 4 boxes in a square on a piece of paper.

Step 2 – label the boxes with your own words to describe:
I have been good at (business)
I have been excellent at (business)
I have been someone to turn to/expert at (business)
I have been rubbish/not so good at (business)

Step 3 – fill the boxes with behaviours related to (business) that fits these labels.

Step 4 – work with a partner and find some floor space to work on.

Step 5 – person B passes their piece of paper to person A with the behaviours listed on the paper.

Step 6 – person B decides where each of the boxes are on the floor (you may wish to use pieces of paper to represent each box) and steps first into 'Rubbish'.

Person A helps person B to think of one of the behaviours and briefly develop the submodalities surrounding that behaviour (sight, sound and feelings). Once person A has seen that person B has experienced that event/behaviour in 'Rubbish', person A instructs person B to move out of that square (it is good to move off this square quickly when person B is in 'state').

This is repeated with each of the boxes in turn, finishing in 'Expert'.

Step 7 - Person A invites person B to move back through the boxes as far as they want to go, since they may not want to experience 'Rubbish'.

Step 8 - This process is repeated with person A following steps 5 onwards.

What have you learnt from this activity?

_____
_____
_____
_____
_____

Chapter 13 – The next steps

'Have confidence that if you have done a little thing well, you can do a bigger thing well too.' – David Storey

During the last twelve chapters, I have shared the secrets of successful performance coaches, who have shared not only their expertise but also their strategies for success. Following this step-by-step process, and remembering to complete the activities as you go, will set you on the route to transforming your coaching business.

Personally, I have learnt a huge amount on this journey. Each of the coaches I interviewed has a unique style although there are also commonalities among them. As a coach, I believe we can take what works for us and develop our own unique strategies for success.

They each had a clear idea of their values, although these did vary. Once you start to understand your values you can create a business that you are passionate about and that gives you purpose, which is the reason why many people enter the profession in the first place. Most importantly, when your business values are aligned with your personal values, you can enjoy what you do every day.

It can be very easy to lack self-belief when running a coaching business, especially during the early stages when you are learning how to coach effectively as well as run a business. Having a strong self-belief and confidence in yourself can transform your success, as you can work to your strengths and get the most out of yourself.

One of the most important aspects that I have learnt

over the last few years is the importance of business skills. However, as you can see, you don't need to have these when you set up your business. You can develop them along the journey. Personally, having a mentor has been the most effective way of developing these skills quickly and easily.

As part of developing the business skills, knowing how to market yourself and how to network effectively is essential. As coaching is a relational business, it is key to build relationships with potential clients, partners and associates. In addition, when you work for yourself, it can be a lonely business, so having that network is essential for your own sanity as well!

Although the jury is still out as to whether coaches should niche, I personally agree that it is easier and simpler if you know your ideal client and how you can target them. But that's not to say that you can't develop and update your niche along your journey too. Even with non-directional coaching, people tend to want to work with someone who is an expert in their field, and it makes sense to work to your strengths and interests.

Like any other business owner, to run a successful business you need a vision of where you want to go. If you don't do this, how are you going to know when you are there? Without a plan you can land up going around in circles, and then you don't create that business that gives you purpose and passion, as well as one that is successful.

That leads on to being aware of how you can continually develop your own skills. As coaches we are work in progress and importantly, employing your own coach or mentor can enable you to further develop your own abilities, your business and ultimately, your success.

Lastly, you can learn from others who do it well and have a determined and positive mindset. Learn from the models who have been interviewed for this book, as well as those who you respect, and find out what works for them. One of the main things that I have learnt is, as much as business and marketing knowledge is essential for running a successful coaching business, having a positive mindset is what keeps you going during the challenging times. And much of this can be sustained and managed by working on yourself. You can change the language you use, the physiology you exhibit and the emotions you feel, which can all be enhanced with the NLP techniques outlined in the book.

So what is next for you? Well firstly, if you haven't yet completed the exercises in the book, I suggest that you go back and do this now. Then start to develop your plan and most importantly – take action.

Your free trial of the Self Discovery Success Club

Now that I have shared the secrets of some of the greatest performance coaches, the next move is up to you. You will go on to continue your own journey of self discovery when you take the next steps to transform your coaching business.

I appreciate that you may not agree with all the information in the book, but many of the coaches have learnt the hard way by making mistakes and if you can avoid these, this is going to enhance your success.

To give you ongoing support and encouragement, I would like to invite you to join me in the Self Discovery Success Club where you will get one month's free trial membership. Just go to:

www.thesecretsofsuccessfulcoaches.com/offer

to claim your membership.

I look forward to seeing you in the club and sharing with you more strategies and tips to accelerate your business even further and to achieve the success you desire.

As quoted by Lao Tzu, 'A journey of a thousand miles begins with a single step,' so take your next step today and enjoy the journey. I wish you every success in creating the amazing business you deserve.

Further resources

For further details on the models interviewed for my book, full details are below. You can also find suggested reading in this section.

- Allison Marlowe, Women's Business Coach, www.allisonmarlowe.com
- Blaire Palmer, Executive Coach, www.blairepalmer.com
- Dawn Breslin, Consciously Female Coach, www.dawnbreslintraining.com
- Duncan Brodie, Leadership Coach, www.goalsandachievements.co.uk
- Gladeana McMahon, Personal Development and Transformational Coach, www.gladeanamcmahon.com
- Hannah McNamara, Marketing Coach, www.marketinghelpforcoaches.com
- Marian Way, Clean Language Coach, www.apricotisland.com
- Michael Neill, Success Coach, www.supercoach.com
- Steve Marriott, Success Coach, www.kaizen-training.com
- Suparna Dhar, Parent Coach, Trainer and Facilitator, www.lifescanvas.co.uk
- Suzy Greaves, Big Leap Coach, www.thebig-leap.com

Suggested reading

- Supercoach: 10 Secrets to Transform Anyone's Life, Neill M, Hay House UK

- Get Clients Now! A 28-Day Marketing Program for Professionals, Consultants, and Coaches, Hayden CJ, Amacon
- Niche Marketing for Coaches, McNamara H, Thorogood
- Achieving Excellence in Your Coaching Practice (Essential Coaching Skills and Knowledge), McMahon G, Palmer S, Wilding C, Routledge
- Coaching for Performance, Whitmore J, Nicholas Brealey Publishing
- The E-Myth Revisited, Gerber M, Harper Business
- Business Stripped Bare: Adventures of a Global Entrepreneur, Branson R, Virgin Books
- Anyone Can Do It: My Story, Bannatyne D, Orion
- Tycoon, Jones P, Hodder Paperbacks
- The Recipe for Success, Palmer B, A&C Black
- Dawn Breslin's Guide to Superconfidence, Breslin D, Hay House UK
- Making The Big Leap, Greaves S, New Holland Publishers Ltd
- Eat That Frog! Get More of the Important Things Done, Today, Tracy B, Mobius
- Discover Yourself on the Yellowbrick Road, Dashwood-Quick W, Lean Marketing Press
- The Monk who sold his Ferrari, Sharma R, Element
- The Aladdin Factor, Canfield J and Hansen MV, Time Warner International
- Follow your Heart, Matthews A, Seashell Publishers
- Unlimited Power, Robbins A, Pocket Books
- The 7 Habits of Highly Effective People, Covey S, Simon & Schuster Ltd